Acknowledgements

I would like to thank my family for all of their support. First to my husband, Dave, for encouraging me to write down these recipes. A special thank you to my son, Michael, and his wife, Kirstin, for providing the opportunity to finally print them in this book. Thank you to all my children: Aaron, Paul, Michael, Nathan and Angela who have been my greatest fans and toughest critics over the years. To my daughters-in-law, Carla and Kirstin, who have loved my sons and enriched their lives!

To my Dad and Mom, Leon and Angela Pietrantonio, for instilling in me the love for family and great food. Thank you Mom for working with me so I could write down some of the family recipes that have never been documented. They will be cherished by our grandchildren and great-grandchildren.

I want to acknowledge my brothers and sister, Angelo, Steve and Cynthia for all of the years of sharing good times together. To my extended family: the Orlando's, Manzo's, D'Amico's, Dastoli's and Pujia's for the time spent with our Zia's and Zio's, as well as our cousins, around the dinner table.

Thanks to Dorothy Lane Market Culinary Center for giving me the opportunity to teach and share my passion for cooking and baking. Working with a professional staff over 10 years has helped me to grow in my confidence and skills.

I am very blessed to have a wonderful family and numerous friends who love and support me!

Table of Contents

Appetizers

Pizza Ricotta

Filling:

16 ounces whole milk ricotta cheese (page 175) drained 1 hour

3 large eggs

2 cups parmesan cheese, grated and packed

¼ teaspoon kosher salt

¼ teaspoon white pepper

Dough:

1 ½ cups flour

2 large eggs

1 teaspoon olive oil

¼ teaspoon kosher salt

Serves 12-15

Filling

For the filling, stir all the ingredients together until it is mixed. Set aside in the refrigerator until ready to assemble.

Dough

Place flour, eggs, oil, and salt in a food processor. Let the machine run for about 30 seconds. A ball of dough will form. If it does not clump or the dough stiffens up very quickly, stop the machine and feel the dough. Adjust for stickiness or dryness by working in either flour or water, 1 teaspoon at a time. Let the machine knead the dough for about 20 seconds, but no more than 40 seconds total processing.

Turn the dough out onto a lightly floured surface and knead by hand for another 30 seconds or until it is a smooth, soft round ball. Wrap in plastic and let rest at room temperature for 30 minutes.

Rolling out pasta dough

Cut the rested ball of pasta dough in 2 pieces. Rewrap the other piece in the plastic wrap so it will not dry out. Have parchment paper on a 12" cookie sheet. Also, have flour for sprinkling and a pizza cutter.

Flatten then sprinkle flour generously on both sides of the piece of dough. Attach a pasta machine to the work surface. Turn the knob to the widest setting (usually #1). Press the first piece of dough with your hands into a small rectangle and roll it through the machine. Roll out from the widest setting (#1) to the thinnest setting (#6) depending on the pasta machine.

Assembly

Cut the long, flattened piece of dough into three pieces, about 12 inches long. Lay all three pieces with sides touching on the parchment lined tray. You will have to press the pieces together at the seams to seal it into one big sheet.

Place the filling on the rolled out dough leaving at least 1" border around the entire edge. Use an off-set spatula to even out the filling. Roll out the other piece of dough into three 12" sheets. Place one sheet on the left. The middle sheet will need 5-6 holes cut with a thimble down the center. Try to have the edges touching. Place the third piece on the remaining part. Press down around the edges to seal the top and bottom dough together. Cut with a ravioli cutter or fluted edge cutter to cut and seal the entire pizza (9" x 11").

Bake at 400 degrees for 30-35 minutes or until golden brown on top. Remove from the oven and allow to cool. Cut into 2" squares.

Ricotta Cheese Cups

30 wonton wrappers

15 ounces whole milk ricotta (page 175) drained 1 hour

3 large eggs

2 cups grated parmesan cheese

¼ teaspoon salt

¼ teaspoon white pepper

Yields 30 cheese cups

Preheat the oven to 375 degrees. Spray 3 mini-muffin tins with cooking spray.

Place each wrapper into a section of a mini-muffin tin. Gently press each wrapper into the muffin cup and arrange so that it forms a cup shape. The wrapper will overlap itself and stick up out of the cup.

In a mixer, on low speed, mix the ricotta, eggs, parmesan cheese, salt and pepper. Spoon about one tablespoon into each cup. Bake for 15-20 minutes on until the tips start to turn golden brown. Remove from muffin tins and serve warm.

Fratonelli (Easter Cheese Puffs)

Dough:

3 cups flour

3 large eggs

3 tablespoons corn oil

¼ cup dry white wine

½ teaspoon salt

Filling:

6 large eggs

3 cups romano cheese, grated

3 cups parmesan cheese, grated

Yields 60

Dough
Mix dough ingredients in a food processor until it comes together into a ball of dough. (Add a tablespoon of wine if dough is too dry.) Remove from bowl and press the dough together until you have a soft smooth ball of dough. Cover with plastic wrap and let rest for 30 minutes before you begin rolling through the pasta roller.

Cut ball of dough into 4-6 pieces. Keep the rest covered until you are ready to use. Flatten and dip each piece of dough into flour on both sides before rolling through the machine set on the widest setting #1 to thinner #5.

Filling
In a medium bowl, mix together the eggs and both the cheeses.

Assembly
Cut into 3 ½ inch rounds. Place one rounded teaspoon of filling across the center and bottom third of the circle; but not too close to the edge. You may brush the edge with a tiny amount of water to help in sealing. Fold over the top and seal with a fork. Place on parchment lined cookie sheets. With a toothpick, poke 5-6 holes into the top of each one (this allows for filling to expand and steam to escape).

Bake at 375 degrees for 10-12 minutes or until lightly golden in color.

Filo Spinach Triangles

2 tablespoons olive oil

1 clove garlic, finely minced

20 ounces fresh baby spinach

15 ounces whole milk ricotta (page 175) drained 1 hour

2 large eggs

2 cups parmesan cheese, grated

1 pound package filo dough, twin pack (thaw following package directions)

1 pound butter, melted

Yields 60 triangles

In a large skillet, heat olive oil and cook garlic for about 30 seconds. Add baby spinach one handful at a time and continue to stir until the spinach is wilted. Season with salt and pepper. Remove from heat and allow to cool. Roughly chop the cooled spinach mixture. In a large bowl, combine the spinach with the ricotta, eggs, and parmesan cheese.

Unroll the filo and lay it flat on a clean, dry surface. Cover completely with plastic wrap or parchment paper. Take two sheets of filo, and keeping the rest covered with the plastic wrap to keep it from drying out, place them vertically in front of you. Brush the filo lightly with butter on a cutting board. Cut the filo lengthwise into thirds. Spoon 1 teaspoon of filling on the lower end of each strip. Fold up the filo strips as you would a flag to create a neat triangle, being careful not to roll too tightly or the triangles will crack when baked. Transfer to a jelly roll pan with sides lined with parchment paper. Place trianlges close together. Brush triangles with more butter. Repeat with the rest of the filo and filling. You can bake the triangles immediately or freeze and bake them later.

To Freeze
Freeze the uncooked triangles in the pan. When frozen, transfer the paper and triangles to an airtight container. If needed, you can store in the freezer for about 1 month.

To Bake
Position racks in the top and bottom thirds of the oven and heat the oven to 375 degrees. Line a sheet pan with parchment paper and arrange the triangles in a single layer on the sheet pan. Bake until golden brown, 20 minutes for fresh and 25 minutes for frozen.

Mushroom Tart

Tart:

1 sheet puff pastry, thawed according to package directions

Mushroom Filling:

2 tablespoons butter

2 tablespoons olive oil

1 large shallot, finely minced

½ of a red bell pepper, chopped

1 pound crimini mushrooms, sliced

1 clove garlic, finely minced

1 tablespoon fresh thyme, leaves only

Salt and pepper to taste

Topping:

⅓ cup parmesan cheese

1 cup shredded asiago fresco cheese

Yields 9 Servings

Tart

Preheat oven to 400 degrees. Unfold the puff pastry sheet on a piece of parchment paper that has been lightly floured. Roll out ¼" bigger than a 12x12 inch square. Fold over the edges ¼" on all sides, crimping with a fork to form a rim. Brush with beaten egg on the edges only. Use a fork to prick the center portion. Bake for 20 minutes or until golden brown. Remove from the oven and allow to cool.

Mushroom Filling

Heat butter and olive oil in a large skillet. Add shallots and red pepper. Cook for about 1 minute. Add the mushrooms and continue to cook until mushrooms are golden brown, about 7 minutes. Add garlic and thyme and stir for 1 minute more. Add salt and pepper to taste. Remove from heat.

You can prepare a day ahead and refrigerate.

Assembly

Preheat the oven to 375 degrees. Place the baked puff pastry on a cookie sheet. Combine the parmesan and shredded asiago cheese and sprinkle on top of the puff pastry. Top with the cooked mushroom filling. Bake for 6-8 minutes or until cheese has melted. Remove and cut into 9 pieces.

Prosciutto Wrapped Rosemary Cheese Straws

1 half pound puff pastry sheet, thawed

1 large egg

¼ cup grated parmesan cheese

2 tablespoons chopped fresh rosemary

14 thin slices of prosciutto, halved lengthwise

1 cantaloupe, sliced

Serves 12-14

Preheat the oven to 400 degrees. Beat the egg in a small bowl with a fork. In another bowl stir the cheese and rosemary together.

Unfold the pastry sheet on a lightly floured surface. Roll the pastry sheet into a 14 x 10 inch rectangle. Cut in half lengthwise. Brush both halves with beaten egg. Sprinkle the cheese mixture on one piece. Place the remaining half on top, egg-side down. Roll gently with a rolling pin to seal.

Cut the pastry crosswise into 24-28 (½ inch) strips. Twist the strips multiple times and place on a baking sheet, pressing down the ends. Brush the pastries with the egg mixture.

Bake for 15-18 minutes or until golden brown. Remove the pastries from the baking sheets and let cool on wire racks for 10 minutes.

Wrap one piece of prosciutto around one cheese straw. Serve with pieces of cantaloupe.

Tip: To make ahead, place the unbaked twists onto a baking sheet and brush with the egg mixture. Cover and freeze until firm. Remove the frozen strips from the baking sheet and store in a gallon size ziplock bag in the freezer for up to 1 month. Bake the frozen pastries on a baking sheet at 400 degrees for 15 minutes or until golden brown.

Roasted Asparagus Wrapped in Prosciutto

12 asparagus stalks (about 1 pound), ends trimmed off

1 tablespoon olive oil

Kosher salt and black pepper

6 slices of prosciutto, halved lengthwise

12 slices parmigiano-reggiano (cut into thin sticks)

1 cantalope, sliced

Serves 6

Preheat the oven to 400 degrees. On a heavy baking sheet, toss the asparagus with the oil, salt and pepper. Place in a single layer on the baking sheet. Roast in the oven until the asparagus is tender, about 10 minutes. Let cool completely.

Place one piece of cheese next to the asparagus and wrap them together with a piece of prosciutto, exposing the tips.

Arrange on a platter and serve at room temperature.

Serve with slices of cantalope.

Roasted Red Pepper Bruschetta

Peppers:

4 red bell peppers

¼ cup extra-virgin olive oil

1 tablespoon fresh Italian parsley, finely minced

1 tablespoon fresh basil, thinly sliced

4 cloves garlic, thinly sliced

Kosher salt and freshly ground pepper to taste

Bruschetta:

8 slices of Italian bread

Kosher salt

2 tablespoons olive oil

Serves 8

Peppers

Place the peppers on the grate of a gas stove on high heat. You may also use a gas grill or place under the broiler. Roast until the skin is charred (black) all around, turning the pepper with a pair of tongs, every 3-5 minutes. The pepper should be evenly blackened on all sides.

Transfer peppers to a bowl and cover tightly with plastic wrap. Let sit (it will steam as it sits) until they are cool enough to handle (about 30 minutes).

Peel off the blackened skin. Cut the peppers in half and remove stem and seeds. Cut the peppers lengthwise into ¼" thick strips.

Place red pepper strips in a medium bowl and stir in olive oil, parsley, basil, garlic, salt and pepper.

Bruschetta

Preheat the oven to 400 degrees. Lightly brush one side of the bread with olive oil and sprinkle with salt. Place brushed side up on a baking sheet and bake for 10 minutes. Remove from oven and cool for a few minutes.

Place roasted red peppers on top of toasted bread immediately before serving.

Stuffed Mushrooms

3 ounces pancetta, chopped

2 tablespoons olive oil

1 large shallot, chopped

16 crimini mushrooms (remove stems and add to other mushrooms)

4 ounces crimini mushrooms, sliced and chop in a food processor with stems

1 clove garlic, finely minced

1 tablespoon fresh parsley, finely chopped

½ cup bread crumbs, plain

¼ cup parmesan cheese, grated

1 large egg

⅔ cup asiago fresco cheese, grated

Serves 8

Preheat the oven to 400 degrees.

Cook pancetta in the olive oil until it starts to brown. Add shallots and continue to cook until shallots are transparent.

Add chopped mushrooms and sauté until tender. Add garlic and stir for 30 seconds. Remove from heat. Stir in parsley and bread crumbs. Once mixture cools, add parmesan cheese and egg.

Place mushrooms on a cookie sheet and divide filling to stuff all of the mushrooms. Top with asiago fresco cheese and bake for 10-15 minutes or until cheese is melted. Remove from oven and transfer to a serving platter.

Puffed Pastry Bundles

1 sheet of puff pastry, thawed

3 slices of proscuitto, cut into thirds

1 package (8 ounces) of marinated small mozzarella balls, cut in half

9 fresh basil leaves

5 sun dried tomatoes, thinly sliced

1 large egg, beaten lightly

¼ cup grated parmesan cheese

Serves 9

Cut the thawed puff pastry (9" x 9" square) into thirds. Cut into thirds again. You should have 9 pieces 3"x3". Place in the middle of each square one piece of prosciutto, 2 pieces of mozzarella, 1 basil leaf (torn into pieces), and ½ of a sliced sun dried tomato.

Roll up the pastry around the cheese mixture and press the seams and pinch the ends to seal. Brush the tops of the rolls with the egg mixture. Dip the tops into the Parmesan cheese. Place the rolls, seam side down onto a baking sheet. Prick the tops of the rolls with a fork.

Preheat the oven to 400 degrees, bake for 25 minutes or until the bundles are golden brown. Remove from the baking sheet and let cool slightly before slicing in half diagonally.

Spinach Pinwheels

10 ounce package frozen
chopped spinach, thawed

1 cup mayonnaise

2 cups sour cream

1 envelope ranch dressing
(powder)

1 bunch green onions, chopped

4 strips of crisply fried bacon,
crumbled

1 package 10" flour tortillas
(package of 8)

Yield: about 50 pieces

The thawed spinach will need to be squeezed tightly to remove the excess water. Mix the spinach, mayo, sour cream, ranch dressing, green onions and bacon together in a bowl. (This can be prepared a day ahead and refrigerated.)

Spread a thin layer of filling on the tortillas all the way around to the edges. Roll up tightly and press gently as you roll. If the filling comes out at the end of tortilla, scrape the excess with a knife and reuse on the next one.

Cover and chill the rolls at least 1 hour or overnight. Slice into ½" slices slightly on the bias. You can get anywhere from 5-8 pieces per tortilla. Gently lay the pinwheels onto a serving tray. The end pieces are too little for a pinwheel.

Pasta Salad

Soup, Salad & Bread

Nonna's Chicken Soup

Broth:

5 quarts cold water, filtered

4-5 pound whole chicken

2 large onion, cut in half

4 celery tops with leaves

2 stalks celery cut in half

2 carrots, whole and peeled

1 large tomato, cut in quarters and seeded

2 cloves garlic, whole and peeled

2 bay leaves

8 stems of fresh parsley

10 peppercorns

1 parmesan cheese rind

Kosher salt to taste

Pastina

1 pound of pastina (tiny pasta)

Soup:

2 tablespoons olive oil

2 carrots, small dice

2 celery stalks, small dice

1 medium onion, finely minced

4 quarts chicken broth

4 cups cooked chicken, diced

Preparing the Broth

Bring the 5 quarts of water and whole chicken to a boil and remove the foam that comes to the top. Keep skimming until all the foam is gone. Add the remaining broth ingredients.

Bring back to a boil and then lower heat to a soft boil or soft bubbling. Do not cover. Cook for 2 hours. Liquid will reduce. Add kosher salt to taste at the end.

Remove the whole chicken and allow to cool before taking apart the chicken, Discard the bones, skin, and fat and cut the meat into pieces and reserve for later use.

Strain the broth through a colander lined with cheese-cloth. Press down to extract as much of the broth in the vegetables. Discard the cheesecloth with the cooked vegetables.

Place the broth in the refrigerator. Once chilled, remove the layer of fat that has solidified on top. (The broth may be refrigerated for 2 days or frozen for up to 3 months.)

Pastina

Bring a 2 quart saucepan with water to a boil. Add salt before cooking according to package directions. It is best to cook "al dente", so pastina is not overcooked. Drain water and add pasta to soup.

Soup

In a large 5 quart saucepan, saute carrots, celery and onion in olive oil until softened. Add the 4 quarts of chicken broth, diced chicken, cooked pastina and the cheese balls.

Cheese Balls:

1 packed cup grated parmesan cheese

1 large egg

¼ teaspoon baking powder

⅓ cup corn oil

Yields 4 quarts of soup and 80 cheese balls

Cheese Balls

Stir parmesan cheese, egg & baking powder together. Roll tiny little balls (about ¼") and place on a parchment paper lined tray. This makes about 80 cheese balls.

Note: If the batter is too wet, add more parmesan cheese. If it is too dry, add a little beaten egg.

In a 10" fry pan, heat up oil. Drop 20 cheese balls into the hot oil. The cheese balls will puff up and expand in size. As soon as they turn golden, flip over and allow the other side to turn golden.

Remove from pan and place in a dish lined with a paper towel, repeat until all are cooked. Drop into hot soup or you can freeze for up to 1 month.

Beef Barley Soup

2 pounds boneless chuck roast or beef stew meat, cut into small cubes

Kosher salt and black pepper

3 tablespoons corn oil

2 cups chopped onions

2 stalks celery, diced

2 whole carrots, diced

1 (6 ounce) can tomato paste

3 medium size cloves garlic, finely minced

1 cup red wine

4 cups water, filtered

6 cups beef broth, low sodium

2 medium sized potatoes, diced

2 bay leaves, 6 stems of thyme, 1 Rosemary stem (wrap in cheesecloth)

12 ounces frozen corn

12 ounces frozen green peas

1 cup barley (quick cooking preferred) follow package directions

Yields 4 quarts of soup

Season beef with Kosher salt and pepper. Place oil in large stock pot. Cook on high to brown the meat (1 pound at a time) on all sides. Repeat with next pound. Remove all of the beef to a bowl and reserve.

Next add the onion, celery, carrots and tomato paste. Once vegetables are softened, add garlic and red wine. Stir all together to remove browned bits off bottom of pan and allow wine to completely evaporate.

Place beef and juices back in the pan and add the water, beef broth and potatoes. Wrap/tie bay leaves and herbs in cheese cloth. Drop it in to the soup. Bring it to a boil. Once it comes to a boil, reduce heat so that it is still bubbling, but softly. Cover with lid and allow soup to cook for 2 hours. Remove lid for an additional 30 minutes and continue to cook until meat is very tender and breaks apart with a fork.

Remove cheese cloth with herbs and discard. Add corn, peas, and cooked barley a few minutes before serving.

Italian Wedding Soup

Meatballs:

¼ pound ground chuck

¼ pound ground pork

2 tablespoons plain bread crumbs

2 tablespoon milk

1 large egg

2 tablespoons grated parmesan cheese

½ teaspoon garlic, finely minced

1 teaspoon parsley, finely minced

Salt and pepper to taste

Soup:

3 tablespoons olive oil

1 medium onion, diced

2 carrots, (small diced)

2 stalks celery, (small diced)

1 clove garlic, finely minced

½ cup white wine

12 cups chicken broth

4 cups cooked chicken, diced

5 ounce bag fresh spinach, roughly chopped

8 ounces pastina (star shaped or orzo)

Yields 12 cups of soup

Meatballs

In a medium bowl combine bread crumb and milk and set aside for 2 minutes. Add the beef, pork, egg, cheese, garlic, parsley and salt/pepper. Mix just until combined. Roll the mixture into small ½" balls or use a melon baller to scoop small meatballs onto a baking sheet. Bake in a 375 degree oven for 8-10 minutes. Once the meatballs are finished baking, add to the soup.

Soup

In an 8 quart stock pot, heat the olive oil. Add the onion, carrots, celery. Cook on high heat stirring until they soften, about 4 minutes. Add the garlic and wine and reduce completely. Add the chicken broth and cooked chicken and bring the stock to a boil. Reduce to a simmer.

Cook the pastina "al dente" in boiling, salted water; drain water and add pastina to the soup. Finally, add the spinach to the simmering soup.

Minestrone with Potatoes, Cabbage & Rice

¼ cup olive oil

1 leek or onion, washed and cut in half then thinly sliced

2 medium potatoes, small dice

2 cloves garlic, finely minced

5 ½ cups chicken broth, divided

1 pound of cabbage (8 cups chopped)

Salt and pepper to taste

1 cup cooked rice (½ cup dry rice with 1 cup water)

2 cups strained tomato sauce or crushed tomatoes

Yields 9 ½ cups

Heat olive oil in an 8 quart stock pot. Add leeks and potatoes and stir for a few minutes until leeks start to turn golden. Stir in garlic for about 30 seconds; then add 1 ½ cups of the chicken broth, the cabbage and salt & pepper to taste. Stir completely to mix up the leeks and potatoes with the cabbage. Cover with a lid and cook on high heat for 10 minutes.

Add the cooked rice, tomato sauce and the rest of the chicken broth. Bring up to a boil; reduce to simmer and cover with a lid and cook for an additional 10 minutes.

Minestrone (Vegetable Soup)

⅓ cup olive oil

1 leek, chopped

3 shallots, finely minced

2 carrots, chopped

2 stalks celery, chopped

2 small zucchini, diced (about 2 cups)

2 garlic cloves, finely minced

2 potatoes, peeled and diced

4 cups green cabbage (Savoy or Regular) shredded

1 (28 ounce) can crushed tomatoes

5 cups chicken or vegetable broth

2 cans (19 ounces) white cannellini beans, drained & rinsed

1 Parmesan cheese rind

2 cups Italian cut green beans, drained

1 cup yellow corn, frozen

1 cup ditilini pasta, cooked "al dente"

Kosher salt and fresh ground black pepper to taste

3 tablespoons fresh basil, finely minced

3 tablespoons fresh parsley, finely minced

Parmesan cheese, freshly grated for serving

Yields 12 cups

Heat olive oil in an 8 quart stock pot. Add the leek, shallots, carrots, celery and zucchini. Stir until they soften, about 4 minutes. Add the garlic and stir for one minute. Add potatoes and cabbage cook, stirring, until the cabbage is wilted, about 5 minutes. Add the tomatoes, broth, beans and parmesan cheese rind and bring to a boil.

Reduce the soup to a simmer and cook covered for 30 minutes. Add the green beans and corn and cook for another 10 minutes. Add cooked ditilini pasta and season with salt and pepper. Add fresh basil and parsley to soup before garnishing with fresh grated parmesan cheese.

Pasta E Fagioli (Pasta & Beans)

½ pound of pancetta, finely diced

¼ cup extra virgin olive oil

1 cup onion, chopped

2 cloves garlic, finely minced

⅓ cup of red wine

1 (28 ounce) can crushed tomatoes

2 cups chicken broth

3 (15.5 ounce) cans cannellini beans (white kidney beans), drained & rinsed

1 teaspoon pesto (page 111)

1 package fresh basil (1 stem, whole)

Salt and pepper to taste

3 tablespoons fresh basil, finely minced

3 tablespoons fresh parsley, finely minced

Garnish with parmesan cheese

½ pound of ditaline pasta (small tubular)

2-3 cups cooking water (saved from water used to boil pasta)

Serves 10-12

In an 8 quart stock pot sauté pancetta in olive oil on high heat until the fat is rendered and it starts to brown. Add onion and cook until softened about 5-6 minutes. Add garlic and stir for 1 minute until you can smell the garlic. Add wine and reduce completely. Add tomatoes, chicken broth, beans, pesto, and one basil stem with leaves. Season with salt and pepper. Bring to a boil, reduce heat to simmer and cover with a lid. Simmer for 30 minutes. Continue to stir frequently so it does not burn.

Take the reserved basil leaves and stack them up and roll them. Thinly slice the leaves and add to tomato mixture as well as the parsley before adding the cooked pasta.

Cook the pasta in salted water according to package directions. Drain pasta but save some of the cooking water. Add the cooked pasta to tomatoes and beans and stir together. Add 2 cups of the cooking water. Add additional pasta water if needed. The consistency should be brothy or loose.

Potato Soup

4 tablespoons butter

¾ cup onion, diced

½ cup celery, diced

½ cup carrots, diced

4 tablespoons flour

6 cups chicken broth

6 medium-large Yukon gold potatoes, peeled and cut into chunks

1 cup half and half

1 cup shredded sharp cheddar cheese

Garnish with crispy bacon bits and freshly chopped chives

Serves 6

In a large saucepan over medium-high heat, melt butter. Cook onion, celery and carrots in butter until softened. Add flour and stir for 2 minutes. Add chicken broth and potatoes and stir all together. Bring to a boil, then cover with a lid. Reduce heat but continue to let it boil for 15-20 minutes, until potatoes are tender. Stir it occasionally so that the potatoes do not stick to the bottom.

With a potato masher, mash potatoes in pan. Stir in half and half and cheese. Bring up to a simmer without boiling and cook, stirring, until thickened, 3-5 minutes.

Garnish each bowl of soup with crispy bacon bits and freshly chopped chives.

Mixed Bean Soup

1 pound bag of 15 mixed beans

2 quarts of water (8 cups)

4 cups chicken broth

2 cups crushed tomatoes

1 Ham bone or 2 ham hocks

2 bay leaves

2 tablespoons butter

2 tablespoons olive oil

1 medium onion, diced (about 1 cup)

1 carrot, small dice

2 stalks celery, small dice

2 cloves garlic, finely minced

5 tablespoons tomato paste

¾ cup white wine

Yields 4 quarts of soup

Place beans in a large pot. Add water 3-4 times the amount of beans. Cover and soak overnight. Drain water and reserve beans.

In an 8 quart sauce pan add the drained beans, 2 quarts of water, chicken broth, crushed tomatoes, ham bone and bay leaves. Place on high heat and bring to a boil.

In a sauté pan add the butter and olive oil. Cook the onion, carrot and celery until they soften. Add the garlic and tomato paste. Keep stirring the tomato paste until all of the vegetables turn red.

Add the wine and allow it to reduce completely. Once wine has reduced, pour vegetables to the 8 quart stock pot.

Bring to a boil and reduce heat so that it is still bubbling, but softly. Simmer uncovered for about 1 ½ hours or until beans are tender. Remove ham bone and let it cool for about 10 minutes. Remove ham from the bone and break into bite-size pieces. Return the pieces of ham to the soup. Taste before adding salt/pepper.

Remove the bay leaves before serving.

Serve with corn bread.

Pasta Salad

1 pound of bow tie pasta or short cut pasta

1 bunch of fresh broccoli, cut into small florettes

1 pound carrots, julienned

1 red bell pepper, diced

8 ounces yellow/orange grape tomatoes

8 ounces red grape tomatoes

12 ounces fresh mozzarella cheese, cubed

2 bunches green onion, thinly sliced at an angle using all the green stems

1 package fresh basil, leaves only thinly sliced

16 ounces Italian salad dressing

Serves 12-15

Cook pasta "al dente" according to package directions and cool down in ice water. Drain and pour pasta in a large bowl. Add all of the vegetables and basil to the pasta. Pour the dressing over the vegetables and pasta. Thoroughly mix together to coat everything with the dressing.

Refrigerate and serve cold.

Baby Greens with Fennel,
Oranges, Dried Cherries & Slivered Almonds

¼ cup extra-virgin olive oil

2 tablespoons balsamic vinegar

1 tablespoon orange marmalade

8 ounces baby greens

1 large fennel bulb, trimmed and finely sliced

4 naval oranges, peel and separated into slices

½ cup dried cherries

½ cup slivered almonds, toasted

Parmesan cheese, shaved

Serves 8

Whisk oil, vinegar and orange marmalade together. Pour over the baby greens and toss together.

Place on top of greens: fennel, a few orange slices, dried cherries and almonds.

Garnish with shavings of parmesan cheese.

Baby Greens with Mandarin
Oranges, Dried Cranberries & Sliced Almonds

¼ cup extra-virgin olive oil

2 tablespoons balsamic vinegar

8 ounces baby greens

1 can (8 ounces) mandarin oranges, drained

½ cup dried cranberries

¼ cup sliced almonds, toasted

Serves 8

Whisk oil and vinegar together. Pour over the baby greens and toss together.

Place mandarin oranges, cranberries and almonds on top.

Romaine Lettuce with Apples & Balsamic Vinaigrette

8 ounces romaine lettuce, torn

¼ cup extra virgin olive oil

2 tablespoons balsamic vinegar

1 extra-large Johnagold or Golden Delicious apple, cut into matchsticks

1 package grape tomatoes

½ of an English cucumber, thinly sliced

Kosher salt and freshly ground black pepper

Serves 8

Place lettuce in a large bowl. Wisk together olive oil and vinegar.

Cut apple into matchstick pieces and place on top of salad along with tomatoes and cucumber slices.

Sprinkle salt and pepper over salad. Pour vinaigrette over salad and toss to evenly coat.

Caprese Salad

8 ounces fresh mozzarella (boc-concini)

8 ounces grape tomatoes

6 fresh basil leaves, sliced into thin ribbons

2 tablespoons olive oil

Kosher salt and freshly ground black pepper

Serves 6

Place mozzarella balls and tomatoes in a serving bowl.

Add basil, olive oil and sprinkle salt and pepper to taste.

Mix together and serve at room temperature.

Cranberry Salad

1 can (20 ounce) crushed pineapple

1 small box (3 ounce) jello (cranberry, raspberry or strawberry)

1 can (15 ounce) jellied cranberry with whole cranberries

1 bag (16 ounces) of fresh cranberries

2 medium apples

Zest of 1 orange, and orange

Serves 12-15

Drain crushed pineapple and reserve the juice. Heat pineapple juice in a 2-cup measuring cup. Microwave for 2 minutes on high heat. Remove and dissolve jello in hot juice. Set aside.

Remove cranberry sauce from the can and place in a larger bowl. Stir the sauce until there are no lumps and it is smooth. Add the crushed pineapple and the jello.

Place fresh cranberries in the food processor and pulse untill finely chopped. Remove and add to the above mixture.

Core and cut apples into 4 pieces and process until finely chopped. Remove and add to the salad.

Remove the zest from the orange and add to the salad. Peel the orange and place the orange segments in the food processor. Process until chopped. Remove and add to the salad.

Refrigerate for at least one hour or overnight is best.

Serve with roast turkey.

Banana Bread

½ cup butter, softened

1 cup sugar

2 large eggs

1 cup mashed bananas

2 cups flour

1 teaspoon baking soda

½ teaspoon salt

½ cup buttermilk

⅔ cup nuts, toasted and rough chopped (walnuts or pecans)

Yields 1 loaf

In a mixer, cream butter and sugar until light and fluffy. Add eggs and bananas. In a separate bowl mix flour, baking soda and salt. Add the flour mixture in two parts, alternating with the buttermilk (flour, milk, flour, milk). Mix until combined, but do not overmix. Fold in nuts.

Cut a piece of parchment paper to fit into the bottom of the loaf pan (9"x5"x2.5"). Spray the entire pan with vegetable spray. Pour the filling into the prepared loaf pan.

Bake at 350 degrees for 60-65 minutes or until a toothpick inserted comes out clean.

Pumpkin Bread

2 cups canned pumpkin

3 cups sugar

1 cup water

1 cup corn or vegetable oil

4 large eggs

3 ½ cups all-purpose flour

2 teaspoons baking soda

1 teaspoon baking powder

2 teaspoons cinnamon

½ teaspoon nutmeg

¾ teaspoon cloves

1 teaspoon salt

Yields 2 loaves

Preheat oven to 350 degrees.

In a bowl, combine the pumpkin, sugar, water, oil and eggs.

In a separate bowl mix the flour, soda, baking powder, spices and salt.

Slowly add the dry mixture to the pumpkin mixture. Whisk together just until incorporated. Do not over mix.

Bake for 1 hour at 350 degrees or until a toothpick comes out clean.

Zucchini Bread

3 large eggs

1 cup corn or vegetable oil

1 ½ cup sugar

2 teaspoons vanilla

2 cups unpeeled zucchini, shredded

8 ounces crushed pineapple in its own juice

3 cups flour

2 teaspoons baking soda

1 teaspoon salt

1 ½ teaspoons cinnamon

¾ teaspoon nutmeg

1 cup nuts, chopped (walnuts or pecans)

Yields 2 loaves

Beat eggs, oil, sugar and vanilla until foamy. Stir in zucchini and pineapple. Add flour, baking soda, salt, cinnamon and nutmeg to wet mixture. Stir just until combined. Fold in the chopped nuts. Pour in two greased and floured loaf pans 9"x5"x2.5".

Bake for 60-65 minutes at 350 degrees or until a toothpick comes out clean.

Garlic Bread

1 large clove garlic, finely minced

2 tablespoons butter

3 tablespoons extra-virgin olive oil

1 French baguette, split in half but still attached

Kosher salt

3 slices of provolone cheese, cut in half

4 tablespoons parmesan cheese, finely grated

1 teaspoon fresh parsley, finely minced

Serves 8-10

Preheat oven to 375 degrees. Combine garlic, butter and olive oil in a microwave safe dish. Heat for 1 minute on high in the microwave.

Brush bread on both cut sides with all of the garlic oil. Lightly sprinkle kosher salt and top with the cheeses. Sprinkle with chopped parsley.

Wrap the entire loaf in foil and place on a cookie sheet. Bake for 15-20 minutes. Slice into diagonal pieces and serve warm.

Soft Pretzels

1 ½ cups fat free milk or water

2 tablespoons corn oil, plus extra for the bowl

1 package active dry yeast

2 tablespoons light brown sugar

4 cups all-purpose flour, plus extra

1 teaspoon salt

Topping:

1 egg, lightly beaten

1 ½ teaspoons Kosher salt

Yield 16 pretzels

Place the milk in a microwave for 45 seconds until lukewarm. Add the oil, yeast and brown sugar. Stir to dissolve the sugar and let rest until foamy, about 5 minutes.

In the bowl of a mixer fitted with a dough hook, add the flour and salt and mix together. Add the milk mixture and mix on low speed until all the flour is incorporated and you have a ball of dough. If the dough is too sticky, add more flour until the ball of dough is smooth. Raise the speed to medium and knead the dough for 3-5 minutes.

Grease a large bowl with a drizzle of oil. Place the dough in the bowl and turn to coat lightly with the oil. Cover and let the dough double in size, about 2 hours. (Option: Place in the refrigerator overnight to rise.)

Preheat the oven to 425 degrees. Line a cookie sheet with parchment paper.

Punch down the dough and remove from the bowl. Divide the dough into 16 pieces. Roll one piece between the palms of your hands and the counter to form a long, thin rope (like a snake) about 18" long. Bring the ends up to form a u-shape and cross one end over the other at the top. Bring the ends down and across each other and press down on the ends to seal.

Place the formed pretzel on the cookie sheet and repeat with the remaining dough. Brush each pretzel with the beaten egg and sprinkle lightly with kosher salt.

Bake until golden brown, 12-15 minutes.

Homemade Pizza

Dough:

1 package active dry yeast

1 ½ cups lukewarm water, filtered

4 cups all-purpose flour (or bread flour)

1 teaspoon table salt

2 tablespoons olive oil, plus a drizzle for the bowl

Pizza Assembly:

2 cups plain tomato sauce

3 teaspoons dried oregano

¾ cup parmesan cheese, grated

12 ounces provolone cheese, grated

12 ounces mozzarella cheese, grated

Yield 3 large pizza

Dough

Place the yeast into the lukewarm water and stir to mix in. Let it stand until it looks foamy on top.

In a food processor, pulse the flour and salt to combine. Pour the water/yeast mixture into the workbowl with the food processor running. Add the olive oil and continue to pulse until it is smooth and elastic, about 30 seconds. Turn the dough onto a lightly floured work surface and shape it into a smooth, round ball. If it is too sticky, add more flour. If too dry, add water until you have a smooth dough.

Place the ball of dough into a bowl that has been lightly greased with olive oil. Cover with plastic wrap and allow it to rise until doubled in size 1 ½-2 hours. Press dough to deflate it. Cut into thirds for 3 large pizzas.

Note: All-purpose flour will give you a chewy crust while bread flour will give you a crisper crust.

Pizza Assembly

Place a pizza stone on the bottom rack and preheat the oven to 500 degrees.

Flatten one ball of dough on parchment paper into a disk with a rolling pin. Roll out to an 11" circle.

Spread plain tomato sauce on the dough, leaving ½" border. Sprinkle dried oregano and your favorite toppings. Sprinkle parmesan, provolone and mozzarella. Slide the pizza onto a baking stone in the oven. Bake until the crust turns brown on the edges and the cheese is melted and golden, 7-10 minutes. Remove to a cutting board and cut into pieces with a pizza cutter.

Cheese Calzones

Dough:

1 pizza dough

Filling:

2 tablespoons olive oil

2 large cloves garlic, minced

¼ teaspoon hot red pepper flakes

1 teaspoon dried oregano

1 pound whole milk ricotta (page 175) drained 1 hour

2 cups provolone cheese, grated

¾ cup parmesan cheese, grated

Kosher salt and black pepper

Topping:

Olive oil for brushing

Kosher salt for sprinkling

Yield 6 large calzone

Dough

Follow the dough section on page 38. Divide the dough into 6 equal pieces. Place each ball of dough onto a piece of parchment paper. Roll each ball into a 9" round.

Filling

In a small pan on medium heat, stir together olive oil, garlic, red pepper flakes and oregano for 1 minute, or until you can smell the garlic. Remove from heat and allow to cool completely.

Stir together the ricotta, provolone, parmesan, oregano, salt and pepper. Add cooled garlic oil and mix in. Cover and refrigerate until needed.

Place a pizza stone on the bottom rack and preheat the oven to 500 degrees.

Assembly

Place about ½ cup of the filling in the center of the bottom half of the rolled out dough. Press the filling in an even layer across the bottom half, leaving a 1" border. Fold the top half over and align the edges. Use a fork to seal the calzone. Cut 5 slits across the top.

Topping

Brush the calzones with olive oil and lightly sprinkle with kosher salt. Slide the calzones onto the baking stone in the oven. Bake until the calzones are golden brown, 11-13 minutes. Remove and cool for 5 minutes.

Angel Hair Pasta

Pasta & Sauces

Fresh Pasta

3 cups unbleached
all-purpose flour

4 large eggs

2 teaspoon olive oil

½ teaspoon salt

**Yields 1 pound of
pasta**

Food Processor Method

Place flour, eggs, oil, and salt in work bowl. Let the machine run for about 30 seconds. A ball of dough will form. If it does not clump or the dough stiffens up very quickly, stop the machine and feel the dough. Adjust for stickiness or dryness by working in either flour or water, 1 teaspoon at a time. Let the machine knead the dough for about 10 seconds, but no more than 40 seconds total processing.

Turn the dough out onto a lightly floured surface and knead by hand for another 30 seconds or until it is a smooth, soft round ball. Wrap in plastic and let rest at room temperature for 30 minutes.

Mixer Method

Place flour, eggs, oil, and salt in mixing bowl of a stand mixer, fitted with paddle attachment. Turn the mixer on low until flour is worked in. Increase speed to 2 and allow the ball of dough to form for 1 minute. If it does not clump or the dough stiffens up very quickly, stop the machine and feel the dough. Adjust for stickiness or dryness by working in either flour or water, 1 teaspoon at a time.

Turn the dough out onto a floured surface and knead by hand for another minute until it is a smooth, soft round ball. Wrap in plastic and let rest at room temperature for 30 minutes.

Hand Method

In a large bowl, combine the flour and salt. Make a well in the center of the flour. Lightly beat the eggs with the oil and pour the mixture into the well. Using a fork, gradually draw the flour into the liquid from the inside wall of the well. Beat gently until the wet mixture forms clumps of flour and dough. Use your hands and begin kneading. Fold the raggedy mass over, pushing and turning it, then folding again. Use the kneading action to clean the sides of the bowl.

When you've formed a ball of dough, place on a lightly floured surface and continue kneading for 2-3 minutes, until the dough is smooth and shiny on the outside, soft throughout (no lumps), and stretchy. If your dough seems too sticky or too hard after it has been kneaded for a minute or two, adjust the consistency with very small amounts of flour or water (1 teaspoon).

Form the dough into a disk, wrap it tightly in plastic wrap, and let it rest at room temperature for 30 minutes. Store, very well wrapped, in the refrigerator for a few hours; or up to 1 month in the freezer. Defrost frozen dough slowly in the refrigerator and let it return to room temperature before rolling. Defrosted dough will need a bit more flour.

Rolling out pasta dough by machine
Cut the rested ball of pasta dough in quarters. Rewrap the other pieces in the plastic wrap so it will not dry out. Have lint-free kitchen towels or parchment paper on trays. Also, have flour for sprinkling and a knife or pastry cutter.

Sprinkle flour generously on both sides of pasta. Attach the pasta machine to the work surface. Turn the knob to the widest setting (#1). Press the first piece of dough with your hands into a small rectangle and roll it through the machine. Follow the rolling fresh pasta instructions and roll out to the thinnest setting (#6) depending on the pasta machine. Cut the long, flattened piece of dough into long sheets that fit on a cutting board. Lay the individual pieces flat on the prepared trays. Roll out the remaining dough following the same instructions.

Tips to keep in mind about dough consistency
Remember that all dough has to rest for 30 minutes before you roll it. Then you can cut the pasta and cook it right away. The dough will soften as it rests. If the dough gets resistant when you start rolling, cover it and let it relax and rest for several minutes. The dough will be soft when you try to roll it. Dip it in flour on both sides before rolling through the rollers.

If the pasta breaks when you put it through the cutters of the pasta machine, it means it was dried too long. If it sticks together when you put it through the cutters, it was not dried or kneaded long enough. Time is important in rolling out dough by hand. If it takes you longer than 8 to 10 minutes, the dough will dry out, lose its pliability and be impossible to thin out.

When the sheet of dough feels like leather on both sides, put it through the cutting blades of the pasta machine: spaghetti or fettuccine. Arrange the noodles in a flat layer on floured parchment paper. Noodles can be cooked immediately or dried and cooked another time. Noodles can be frozen for up to one month.

Fresh Spinach Pasta

2 cups packed fresh spinach, stems removed and then rough chop

2 large eggs

2 teaspoons olive oil

½ teaspoon table salt

3 cups unbleached all-purpose flour, or a little more

Yields 1 pound of Pasta

To make the spinach pasta dough, put the spinach, eggs, olive oil and salt in a food processor and puree until smooth. Scrape the green puree down into the bowl.

Add the flour and process again until a ball of dough forms or dough sticks together when you pinch it. If the dough seems too sticky, sprinkle with a little more flour and knead some more.

Wrap the dough in plastic and set aside on the counter to rest for 30 minutes.

Fresh Semolina Pasta

1 ½ cups all-purpose flour

1 ½ cups pasta flour (golden semolina and extra fancy durum)

5 large eggs

1 tablespoons olive oil

½ teaspoon table salt

Yields 1 pound of Pasta

Pour both flours into a large bowl. Make a well in the center of the flour and pour in the eggs, olive oil and salt. Using a fork, begin to gradually incorporate the flour, starting with the inner rim and scrambling the eggs.

Try to pull the flour in slowly and keep it around the edge of the bowl. Once half the flour has been mixed in and the mixture has formed a shaggy mass, transfer the dough to a work surface.

Place all of the loose flour to the side and begin to knead the dough. Keep incorporating the flour by folding and kneading.

Use the heel of your palm to push the dough down and away, then fold the edge back over top to keep a round dough ball. Rotate the dough each time you knead it.

Continue kneading the dough about 5 minutes or until the dough is a smooth ball. When you squeeze the dough, it should release easily from your fingers without dough sticking to them. Knead in a little flour if it is too sticky.

The small bubbles that start to appear on the surface are a sign that the gluten has developed completely and the dough has been kneaded enough.

Cover the dough with plastic wrap and allow it to rest for 30 minutes at room temperature before rolling.

Lemon Pepper Fettuccine

Pasta Dough:

3 cups unbleached all-purpose flour

4 large eggs

2 teaspoons olive oil

½ teaspoon salt

1 tablespoon fresh ground black pepper

Zest and juice of one lemon

Brown Butter/Fresh Herb Sauce:

12 tablespoons butter (1 ½ sticks)

1 tablespoon fresh thyme, finely minced

1 tablespoon fresh rosemary, finely minced

1 tablespoon fresh sage, finely minced

1 tablespoon fresh parsley, finely minced

Zest of one lemon

Fresh grated parmesan cheese for garnish

Yields 1 pound of Pasta

Pasta Dough

Mix all together in a food processor until dough looks like wet sand pebbles or comes together in a ball of dough. If it is too sticky, add a few tablespoons of flour. If it is too dry and will not stick together, add a tablespoon of water and process for a few seconds until it looks like wet sand pebbles that will stick together.

Remove dough from the food processor and gather into a ball. Cover with plastic wrap and allow to rest for 30 minutes at room temperature.

Rolling out pasta dough by machine

Cut the rested ball of pasta dough in 4 pieces. Rewrap the other pieces in the plastic wrap so they will not dry out. Have parchment paper spread on trays. Also, have flour for sprinkling and a pizza cutter.

Sprinkle flour generously on both sides of pasta. Attach the pasta machine to the work surface. Turn the knob to the widest setting (#1). Press the first piece of dough with your hands into a small rectangle and roll it through the machine. Follow the rolling fresh pasta instructions and roll out to #5 depending on the pasta machine or how thick you want your pasta. Cut the long, flattened piece of dough into two pieces, 12" long. Lay the cut pieces flat on the prepared trays. Roll out the remaining dough following the same instructions. Now check after 5-10 minutes to see if the pasta is drying out and feels like leather. If it does, flip over each sheet of pasta so that the other side can dry out. Check after 5-10 minutes to see if the top has dried out a little. The pasta should be ready to run through the fettuccine cutter.

If the pasta will not run through the fettuccine cutter, it means it has cracked and dried on the edge. You will need to cut the edge off and try running it through again.

If the pasta breaks when you put it through the cutters of the pasta machine, it means it was dried too long. If it sticks together when you put it through the cutters, it was not dried or kneaded long enough.

Time is important in rolling out dough by hand. If it takes you longer than 8-10 minutes, the dough will dry out, lose its pliability and be impossible to thin out.

When the sheet of dough is no longer sticky, put it through the fettuccine cutter on the pasta machine. Arrange the noodles in a flat layer on floured parchment paper. Noodles can be cooked immediately or dried and cooked another time. Noodles can be frozen for up to one month.

Brown Butter/Fresh Herb Sauce
Heat a large skillet over medium heat and melt the butter. To brown the butter, cook on low to medium heat. You will need to swirl the pan or keep stirring the butter until the white butter solids turn golden at the bottom of the pan. Remove from heat and add the fresh herbs and lemon zest, swirling them in the butter.

Cook the pasta in salted boiling water and drain and toss in with the butter sauce. Top with fresh grated parmesan cheese.

Marinara Sauce

⅔ cup extra virgin olive oil

1 medium onion, finely minced

1/2 red bell pepper, finely minced

3 cloves garlic, finely minced

1 cup white or red wine

2 (26-32 ounce) strained or crushed tomatoes

1 can (14 ounce) chicken broth or vegetable broth

1 tablespoon pesto (page 111)

1 package (¾ ounce) fresh basil (reserve 1 stem with leaves attached)

Kosher salt and freshly ground pepper, to taste

Yields 7 cups of sauce

Heat the olive oil in a large saucepan on medium-high heat. Saute the onions and red pepper for about 5 minutes until they are softened. Add garlic and wine and allow the wine to completely reduce.

Add tomatoes, chicken broth, red bell pepper, and pesto. Add one stem of basil, reserving the other for later. Season with salt and pepper.

Bring to a boil and reduce heat so that the sauce softly bubbles. Continue cooking for 30 minutes or until sauce thickens and reduces. Frequently stir to prevent the bottom of the pan from burning. Remove the cooked basil stem.

Take reserved basil stem and remove all the leaves. Stack the leaves on top of each other and cut thin ribbons of basil. Add to the sauce once it is finished cooking.

Tomato Sauce (With Meat)

1 pound of boneless pork meat (country style ribs)

Kosher salt and black pepper

⅔ cup extra virgin olive oil

1 medium onion, chopped

4 cloves garlic, finely minced

1 cup white or red wine

1 can whole peeled tomatoes (28 ounce), hand crush

1 can chicken broth (14 ounces)

1 tablespoon pesto (page 111)

1 red pepper, cut in half with seeds and stem removed

1 Parmesan cheese rind

1 package (¾ ounce) fresh basil (reserve 1 stem with leaves attached)

2 (26-32 ounce) strained or crushed tomatoes

Cooked meatballs (see Mary's Meatball recipe on page 100)

Yields 10 cups of sauce

Season pork meat with salt and pepper. Heat the olive oil in a large stock pan and cook meat until it is brown on both sides. Add onion and cook for about 5 minutes or until onion is transparent. Add garlic and stir then add wine and allow it to completely reduce.

Pour in tomatoes, chicken broth, pesto, red pepper and cheese rind. Add package of basil, reserving the one stem for later.

Continue cooking on medium heat for 30 minutes. Once tomatoes have broken down, add the crushed tomatoes. Cook on low-medium heat for 45 minutes. Add meatballs and cook for 20-30 more minutes. Remove the meatballs so that they are not overcooked. Continue to stir to prevent scorching on the bottom of the pan. Remove the cooked basil stems and the red pepper.

Take reserved basil stem and remove the leaves from the stems. Stack the leaves on top of each other and cut thin ribbons of basil. Add to the sauce once you have removed the pork meat and meatballs.

Serve with your favorite pasta.

Abruzzo Ravioli

Ravioli Filling:

1 tablespoon olive oil

1 clove garlic, finely minced

5 ounce bag of baby spinach

2 tablespoons olive oil

1 small shallot, finely minced

6 baby carrots, grated

1¼ pounds ground veal

1 clove garlic, finely minced

½ cup white wine

Salt and pepper to taste

2 large eggs

1 cup grated parmesan cheese

¼ cup fresh parsley, finely chopped

1 Pound Fresh Pasta (page 42)

Marinara Sauce (page 48)

Yields 50 ravioli/5 servings

Ravioli Filling

In a 12" sauté pan heat garlic in the oil until sizzling. Add all of the baby spinach and stir until wilted. Add a pinch of Kosher salt and freshly ground pepper. Remove from heat and cool. Once cooled, finely chop spinach. Reserve for later.

In a 12" sauté pan heat olive oil and add shallots and carrots and cook until shallots are transparent. Add the ground veal and stir to break up. Season with salt and pepper. Cook until no longer pink. Add the garlic and wine and allow the wine to evaporate. Remove from heat and allow to cool. Add the cooled/chopped spinach. Mix in the eggs, parmesan cheese and parsley and refrigerate.

Fresh Pasta Dough

1 pound Fresh Pasta (see "Fresh Pasta" on page 42-43).

Sauce

1 batch of Marinara sauce (see "Marinara Sauce" on page 48).

Assembly

Cut the fresh pasta dough into 4 pieces. Take out one piece and leave the rest covered in plastic. Flatten the piece and coat the entire piece with flour before rolling through the widest setting (#1) on the pasta machine. Roll out the piece of dough to the thinnest setting (#6). The sheet will be very thin. Do not add any more flour. You want the sheet to be slightly tacky. You will need to cut, stuff, and shape each sheet as soon as the dough is rolled out. Keep your surface floured well so that the ravioli do not stick to the counter or surface you are making them on.

Cut the sheet in half and lay it down on parchment paper.

Place a full teaspoon of filling on bottom half every two inches. You should be able to make seven mounds. Fold the empty dough over the filling, aligning the edges and seal the dough around each mound of filling, pressing out any air pockets with your finger-tips. Cut the dough between each mound of filling into individual ravioli and press the edges to seal. Place on parchment lined trays that are lightly floured and do not let the ravioli touch.

Note: Ravioli can be kept refrigerated for a few hours or it can be frozen on the tray. Once frozen, place in a freezer bag. Keep frozen for no more than 2 months.

Cooking Ravioli
Bring a large pot of water to a boil and add salt. Once water is boiling, add half the ravioli and stir. Cook for 1-2 minutes. Ravioli will rise to the top of the pan when they are done. Push them down and stir until all have risen. Drain in a colander and place in serving dish. Add sauce and stir to coat. Repeat with the other half of the ravioli.

Chicken Marsala Ravioli with Mushroom Cream Sauce

Ravioli Filling:

1½ pounds boneless chicken breast, cut into thin strips

Kosher salt and fresh ground pepper

2 tablespoons olive oil

2 tablespoons butter

½ cup dry Marsala wine

1 large clove garlic, finely minced

2 large eggs

½ cup provolone cheese, grated

¼ cup parmesan cheese

2 tablespoons fresh parsley, finely chopped

Extra parsley, finely chopped for garnishing

1 Pound Fresh Pasta (page 42)

Ravioli Filling
Season chicken strips on both sides with kosher salt and pepper. Heat oil and butter in a 12" fry pan and sear meat on one side without stirring for two minutes. Once meat has caramelized on the first side, flip all the pieces over and add the wine. Allow the liquid to completely evaporate, stir the pieces and reduce heat to medium high. Add the garlic and stir for 30-60 seconds. Remove from heat and allow to cool.

Place cooled meat in food processor and pulse until it resembles finely chopped meat. Place in another bowl and add the eggs, cheeses and parsley. Mix together and set aside.

Fresh Pasta Dough
1 pound Fresh Pasta (see "Fresh Pasta" on page 42-43).

Assembly
Cut the fresh pasta dough into 4 pieces. Take out one piece and leave the rest covered in plastic. Flatten the piece and coat the entire piece with flour before rolling through the widest setting (#1) on the pasta machine. Roll out the piece of dough to the thinnest setting (#6). The sheet will be very thin. Do not add any more flour. You want the sheet to be slightly tacky. You will need to cut, stuff, and shape each sheet as soon as the dough is rolled out. Keep your surface floured well so that the ravioli do not stick to the counter or surface you are making them on.

Mushroom Cream Sauce:

3 tablespoons olive oil

3 tablespoons butter

1 pound crimini mushrooms, sliced and roughly chopped (or baby Portobello mushrooms)

2 large shallots, chopped

Salt and pepper to taste

1 garlic clove, finely minced

½ cup dry Marsala wine

1 ½ cups heavy cream

Garnish with fresh parsley, finely minced

Yields 50 ravioli/5 servings

Cut the sheet in half and lay it down on parchment paper.

Place a full teaspoon of filling on bottom half every two inches. You should be able to make seven mounds. Fold the empty dough over the filling, aligning the edges and seal the dough around each mound of filling, pressing out any air pockets with your fingertips. Cut the dough between each mound of filling into individual ravioli and press the edges to seal. Place on parchment lined trays that are lightly floured and do not let the ravioli touch.

Mushroom Cream Sauce
In a large sauté pan, heat olive oil and butter. Add the mushrooms and cook 5 minutes until slightly softened. Add shallots and cook an additional 2 minutes. Add salt, pepper, garlic and marsala wine. Allow wine to completely reduce; then pour in heavy cream and bring to a boil. Turn heat down to medium-low. When the sauce has reduced by half remove from heat. Stir in fresh parsley and immediately serve with chicken marsala ravioli.

Cooking Ravioli
Bring a large pot of water to a boil and add salt. Once water is boiling, add half the ravioli and stir. Cook for 1-2 minutes. Ravioli will rise to the top of the pan when they are done. Push them down and stir until all have risen. Drain in a colander and place in serving dish. Add sauce and stir to coat. Repeat with the other half of the ravioli.

Butternut Squash Ravioli
with Browned Butter & Gremolata

Ravioli Filling:

1 Butternut squash (about 2 ½ pounds), halved and seeded

1 cup mascarpone cheese

⅓ cup finely grated Parmesan cheese, plus more for garnish

1 tablespoon lemon zest

¼ teaspoon fresh grated nutmeg

Kosher salt and white pepper to taste

1 Pound Fresh Pasta (page 42)

Browned Butter and Gremolata Sauce:

12 tablespoons (1 ½ sticks) unsalted butter

⅓ cup pine nuts

1 tablespoon finely minced sage

1 tablespoon finely minced parsley

1 tablespoon lemon zest

1 small clove garlic, finely minced

Yields 50 ravioli/5 servings

Ravioli Filling

Preheat oven to 425 degrees. Place squash on a baking sheet (cut side down) and roast until soft, about 45-50 minutes. Scoop out flesh leaving the skin. It should measure about 2 ½ cups of squash. Pulse in a food processor. Add the mascarpone, parmesan cheese, lemon zest, nutmeg, salt and pepper. Pulse until smooth. Allow filling to cool before placing in ravioli. (This can be made a couple of days ahead.)

Browned Butter & Gremolata Sauce

Melt butter in a large saute pan over medium high heat. Reduce heat to medium until the butter starts to bubble and foam, about 5 minutes, stirring frequently. Continue cooking until the foam subsides and brown specks start to appear. Turn off heat. Stir in the pine nuts, sage, parsley, zest and garlic. Cover with a lid to keep warm while you cook the ravioli.

Assembly

Cut the fresh pasta dough into 4 pieces. Take out one piece and leave the rest covered in plastic. Flatten the piece and coat the entire piece with flour before rolling through the widest setting (#1) on the pasta machine. Roll out the piece of dough to the thinnest setting (#6). The sheet will be very thin. Do not add any more flour. You want the sheet to be slightly tacky. You will need to cut, stuff, and shape each sheet as soon as the dough is rolled out.

Keep your surface floured well so that the ravioli do not stick to the counter or surface you are making them on. Cut the sheet in half and lay it down on parchment paper.

Place a full teaspoon of filling on bottom half every two inches. You should be able to make seven mounds. Fold the empty dough over the filling, aligning the edges and seal the dough around each mound of filling, pressing out any air pockets with your finger-tips. Cut the dough between each mound of filling into individual ravioli and press the edges to seal. Place on parchment lined trays that are lightly floured and do not let the ravioli touch.

Cooking Ravioli
Bring a large pot of water to a boil and add salt. Once water is boiling, add half the ravioli and stir. Cook for 1-2 minutes. Ravioli will rise to the top of the pan when they are done. Push them down and stir until all have risen. Drain in a colander and place in serving dish. Add sauce and stir to coat. Repeat with the other half of the ravioli.

Chicken & Prosciutto Ravioli

Ravioli Filling:

1 ½ pounds boneless chicken breast

1 tablespoon fresh rosemary, chopped

Kosher salt and fresh ground pepper

2 tablespoons olive oil

⅓ cup white wine

1 large clove garlic, finely minced

¼ pound thinly sliced prosciutto, tear into pieces

3 large eggs

½ cup grated parmesan cheese

2 tablespoons fresh parsley, finely chopped (plus more for garnishing)

1 Pound Fresh Pasta (page 42)

Marinara Sauce (page 48)

Yields 50 ravioli/5 servings

Ravioli Filling

Cut chicken into strips so that they cook quickly. Season with kosher salt, pepper and rosemary on both sides. Heat oil in a 12" fry pan and sear meat on one side without stirring for two minutes. Once chicken has browned on the first side, flip all the pieces over and add the wine. Allow the liquid to completely evaporate, stir the pieces and reduce heat to medium high. Add the garlic and stir for 30-60 seconds. Remove from heat and allow to cool.

Place slightly cooled chicken and prosciutto in a food processor and pulse until it resembles finely chopped meat. Do not over-process or you will have paste. Place in another bowl and add the eggs, cheese and parsley. Mix together and set aside. This can be made a day ahead.

Sauce
1 batch of Marinara Sauce (see "Marinara Sauce" on page 48)

Assembly
Cut the ball of dough into 4 pieces. Take out one piece and leave the rest covered in plastic. Flatten the piece and coat the entire piece with flour before rolling through the widest setting (#1) on the pasta machine. Roll out the piece of dough to the thinnest setting (#6). The sheet will be very thin. Do not add any more flour.

You want the sheet to be slightly tacky. You will need to cut, stuff, and shape each sheet as soon as the dough is rolled out. Keep your surface floured well so that the ravioli do not stick to the counter or surface you are making them on. Cut the sheet in half and lay it down on parchment paper.

Place a full teaspoon of filling on bottom half every two inches. You should be able to make seven mounds. Fold the empty dough over the filling, aligning the edges and seal the dough around each mound of filling, pressing out any air pockets with your fingertips. Cut the dough between each mound of filling into individual ravioli and press the edges to seal. Place on parchment lined trays that are lightly floured and do not let the ravioli touch.

Cooking Ravioli

Bring a large pot of water to a boil and add salt. Once water is boiling, add half the ravioli and stir. Cook for 1-2 minutes. Ravioli will rise to the top of the pan when they are done. Push them down and stir until all have risen. Drain in a colander and place in serving dish. Add sauce and stir to coat. Repeat with the other half of the ravioli.

Crab Ravioli

Ravioli Filling:

1 pound lump crab

1 Pound Fresh Spinach Pasta (page 44)

Creamy Tomato Sauce:

3 tablespoons unsalted butter

1 shallot, finely minced

2 cloves garlic, finely minced

½ teaspoon red pepper flakes

½ pound uncooked shrimp. medium sized

1 cup heavy cream

1 cup plain tomato sauce

⅔ cup grated parmesan cheese

Small red pepper dice and fresh parsley, minced for garnishing the plate

Yields 50 ravioli/5 servings

Creamy Tomato Sauce
Melt butter on medium high heat. Add shallot, garlic, red pepper flakes and shrimp. Cook shrimp for just 1 minute on one side and flip over; add the heavy cream. Allow to reduce slightly. Add the tomato sauce and parmesan cheese. Cook until just heated. Do not boil. Set aside until ready to pour over crab ravioli.

Fresh Spinach Pasta Dough
1 pound Fresh Spinach Pasta (see "Fresh Spinach Pasta" on page 44)

Assembly
Cut the ball of dough into 4 pieces. Take out one piece and leave the rest covered in plastic. Flatten the piece and coat the entire piece with flour before rolling through the widest setting (#1) on the pasta machine. Roll out the piece of dough to the thinnest setting (#6). The sheet will be very thin. Do not add any more flour. You want the sheet to be slightly tacky. You will need to cut, stuff, and shape each sheet as soon as the dough is rolled out. Keep your surface floured well so that the ravioli do not stick to the counter or surface you are making them on.

Cut the sheet in half and lay it down on parchment paper. Place a full teaspoon of filling on the bottom half every two inches. You should be able to make seven mounds. Fold the empty dough over the filling, aligning the edges and seal the dough around each mound of filling, pressing out any air pockets with your fingertips. Cut the dough between each mound of filling into individual ravioli and press the edges to seal. Place on parchment lined trays that are lightly floured and do not let the ravioli touch.

Cooking Ravioli

Bring a large pot of water to a boil and add salt. Once water is boiling, add half the ravioli and stir. Cook for 1-2 minutes. Ravioli will rise to the top of the pan when they are done. Push them down and stir until all have risen. Drain in a colander and place in serving dish. Add sauce and stir to coat. Repeat with the other half of the ravioli.

Giant Asparagus Ravioli with Soft Cooked Egg

Ravioli Filling:

1 pound thin green asparagus

3 tablespoons unsalted butter

1 clove garlic, finely minced

6 scallions, thinly slice white and some of the green

¾ pound fresh thick whole milk ricotta cheese (page 175) drained 2 hours

2 ounces grated parmesan cheese (1 cup), plus extra for serving

½ cup soft white bread crumbs

zest of 1 lemon

1 large egg yolk

Kosher salt, white pepper, and freshly grated nutmeg to taste

12 large eggs, cold (so the yolk won't tend to break open)

1 Pound Fresh Pasta (page 42)

Brown Butter Sauce:

½ cup unsalted butter

Zest and juice of 1 lemon

½ package fresh sage leaves

Yields 12 large ravioli

Ravioli Filling

Trim the tough ends from the asparagus. Slice into 2" pieces. Heat the butter and garlic in a skillet. Add the cut asparagus and scallions and saute over high heat until the asparagus is brightly colored and crisp-tender, about 2 minutes. Remove from the heat and cool, then finely chop by hand or place in a bowl of a food processor.

Combine the asparagus mixture with the ricotta, parmesan cheese, bread crumbs, lemon zest and egg yolk in a medium bowl. Mix well, and season to taste with Kosher salt, white pepper, and nutmeg. The filling should be firm enough to hold its shape.

Transfer the filling to a piping bag or a heavy-duty zip bag and cut a hole out of one corner about the thickness of a pencil. Reserve in the refrigerator. (Filling may be made 1 day ahead.)

Brown Butter Sauce

Heat a 10" skillet over medium heat and melt the butter. To brown the butter, cook on low to medium heat. You will need to swirl the pan or keep stirring the butter until the white butter solids turn golden at the bottom of the pan. Add the lemon zest, juice and sage leaves. The leaves will sizzle and flavor the browned butter. Remove from the heat and spoon on top of the large ravioli.

Assembly

Cut the fresh pasta dough into 4 pieces. Take out one piece and leave the rest covered in plastic. Flatten the piece and coat the entire piece with flour before rolling through the widest setting (#1) on the pasta machine. Roll out the piece of dough to the thinnest setting (#6). The sheet will be very thin. Do not add any more flour. You want the sheet to be slightly tacky. You will need to cut, stuff, and shape each sheet as soon as the dough is rolled out. Keep your surface floured well so that the ravioli do not stick to the counter or surface you are making them on. Cut the pasta sheet in half and lay it down on parchment paper.

Using a pizza cutter, cut about a 4" square of dough. Remove the bag of filling from the refrigerator and pipe a circle of filling about 4/10" from the edge of the dough, leaving a hole in the center. Pipe another layer of filling over the first layer creating about 1" of filling with the center void of filling. Carefully break open 1 egg, separating the yolk from the white. Carefully place the yolk into the center ring. Drape a larger piece of dough (6" square) on top of the filled ravioli to accommodate the height.

Press the dough around the mound of filling while at the same time pushing out any air pockets. Press and cut the outside edges firmly with a fluted pastry cutter or ravioli cutter to ensure they are well sealed.

Cooking Ravioli

Bring a large pot of water to a boil and add salt. Once water is boiling, add 1 or 2 ravioli and stir gently. Cook for 4-5 minutes. A slotted spoon will help you carefully remove and drain the cooked ravioli.

Place in serving dish. Top with brown butter sauce and grated parmesan cheese.

Meat Ravioli

Ravioli Filling:

¾ pound boneless chicken breast

¾ pound boneless pork loin

1 tablespoon fresh rosemary, chopped

Kosher salt and fresh ground pepper

2 tablespoons olive oil

½ cup white wine

1 large clove garlic, finely minced

3 large eggs

½ cup grated parmesan cheese

2 tablespoons fresh parsley, finely chopped

1 Pound Fresh Pasta (page 42)

Marinara Sauce (page 48)

Yields 50 ravioli/5 servings

Ravioli Filling

Cut both meats into strips so that they cook quickly. Season with Kosher salt, pepper and rosemary on both sides. Heat oil in a 12" fry pan and sear meat on one side without stirring for two minutes. Once meat has caramelized on the first side, flip all the pieces over and add the wine. Allow the liquid to completely evaporate, stir the pieces and reduce heat to medium high. Add the garlic and stir for 30-60 seconds. Remove from heat and allow to cool.

Place cooled meat in food processor and pulse until it resembles finely chopped meat. Place in another bowl and add the eggs, cheese and parsley. Mix together and set aside.

Assembly

Cut the fresh pasta dough into 4 pieces. Take out one piece and leave the rest covered in plastic. Flatten the piece and coat the entire piece with flour before rolling through the widest setting (#1) on the pasta machine. Roll out the piece of dough to the thinnest setting (#6). The sheet will be very thin. Do not add any more flour. You want the sheet to be slightly tacky. You will need to cut, stuff, and shape each sheet as soon as the dough is rolled out. Keep your surface floured well so that the ravioli do not stick to the counter or surface you are making them on. Cut the pasta sheet in half and lay it down on parchment paper.

Place a full teaspoon of filling on bottom half every two inches. You should be able to make seven mounds. Fold the empty dough over the filling, aligning the edges and seal the dough around each mound of filling, pressing out any air pockets with your fingertips. Cut the dough between each mound of filling into individual ravioli and press the edges to seal. Place on parchment lined trays that are lightly floured and do not let the ravioli touch.

Cooking Ravioli
Bring a large pot of water to a boil and add salt. Once water is boiling, add half the ravioli and stir. Cook for 1-2 minutes. Ravioli will rise to the top of the pan when they are done. Push them down and stir until all have risen. Drain in a colander and place in serving dish. Add sauce and stir to coat. Repeat with the other half of the ravioli.

Pumpkin Ravioli with Brown Butter Sage

Ravioli Filling:

4 tablespoons butter

⅓ cup minced shallots

2 cups pumpkin puree

⅓ cup heavy cream

⅓ cup parmesan cheese, grated

⅛ teaspoon grated nutmeg

Salt and pepper to taste

1 Pound Fresh Pasta (page 42)

Brown Butter Sage Sauce:

12 tablespoons butter

1 package fresh sage leaves, stems removed

⅓ cup pine nuts

Parmesan cheese for grating on top

Yields 50 ravioli/5 servings

Ravioli Filling

In a large saute pan, over medium heat, melt the butter. Add the shallots and saute for 1 minute. Add the pumpkin puree and cook until the mixture is slightly dry, about 5 minutes. Season with salt and pepper. Stir in the cream and continue to cook for 5 minutes. Remove from the heat and stir in the cheese and grated nutmeg.

Brown Butter Sage Sauce

Heat a large skillet over high heat and melt the butter. To brown the butter, cook on low to medium heat. You will need to swirl the pan or keep stirring the butter until the white butter solids turn golden at the bottom of the pan. If some of the sage leaves are large, cut in half or thirds. Add the sage leaves and pine nuts, swirling them in the butter which will cook them. Pour over the cooked pumpkin ravioli. Before serving, sprinkle with the grated parmesan cheese.

Assembly

Cut the fresh pasta dough into 4 pieces. Take out one piece and leave the rest covered in plastic. Flatten the piece and coat the entire piece with flour before rolling through the widest setting (#1) on the pasta machine. Roll out the piece of dough to the thinnest setting (#6). The sheet will be very thin. Do not add any more flour. You want the sheet to be slightly tacky. You will need to cut, stuff, and shape each sheet as soon as the dough is rolled out. Keep your surface floured well so that the ravioli do not stick to the counter or surface you are making them on.

Cut the sheet in half and lay it down on parchment paper. Working quickly, place a full teaspoon of filling on the bottom half every two inches. You should be able to make seven mounds. Fold the empty dough over the filling, aligning the edges and seal the dough around each mound of filling, pressing out any air pockets with your fingertips. Cut the dough between each mound of filling into individual ravioli and press the edges to seal. Place on parchment lined trays that are lightly floured and do not let the ravioli touch.

Cooking Ravioli

Bring a large pot of water to a boil and add salt. Once water is boiling, add half the ravioli and stir. Cook for 1-2 minutes. Ravioli will rise to the top of the pan when they are done. Push them down and stir until all have risen. Drain in a colander and place in serving dish. Add sauce and stir to coat. Repeat with the other half of the ravioli.

Ricotta & Spinach Ravioli

Ravioli Filling:

2 tablespoons olive oil

2 small shallots or onion, minced

2 cloves garlic, finely minced

10 ounce bag fresh spinach

16 ounces whole milk ricotta (page 175) drained 2 hours

1 cup parmesan cheese, grated

2 large eggs

Kosher salt and black pepper

Simple Tomato Sauce:

¼ cup olive oil

½ cup minced onion (1 small onion)

2 garlic cloves, finely minced

(26-32 ounce) strained tomatoes or crushed tomatoes

1 teaspoon pesto (page 111)

1 package (¾ ounce) fresh basil, divided in half

½ teaspoon Kosher salt/freshly ground pepper

1 Pound Fresh Pasta (page 42)

Yields 50 ravioli/5 servings

Ravioli Filling

Heat olive oil in a large skillet and add the shallot/onion and sauté until translucent. Add the garlic and stir for 20 seconds. Add a large handful of fresh spinach and stir until wilted. Continue to add handfuls of spinach and stir until wilted and all spinach is used. Add salt and pepper to taste and allow to cool completely. With a knife, chop the spinach up before adding to the ricotta.

Mix all ingredients together and refrigerate.

Simple Tomato Sauce

Heat oil and add onion. Sauté for 3-5 minutes. Add garlic and stir for 1 minute. Add the tomatoes, pesto, 1 stem of basil, salt, and pepper. Cook, uncovered on medium heat for 8-10 minutes, stirring occasionally. Discard cooked basil. With the remaining basil, stack the leaves and slice into thin strips and add to the finished sauce.

Assembly

Cut the fresh pasta dough into 4 pieces. Take out one piece and leave the rest covered in plastic. Flatten the piece and coat the entire piece with flour before rolling through the widest setting (#1) on the pasta machine. Roll out the piece of dough to the thinnest setting (#6). The sheet will be very thin. Do not add any more flour. You want the sheet to be slightly tacky. You will need to cut, stuff, and shape each sheet as soon as the dough is rolled out.

Cut the sheet in half and lay it down on parchment paper. Apply a little water with a brush on the bottom half of pasta sheet. This will hold it together. Place a full teaspoon of filling on bottom half every two inches. You should be able to make seven mounds. Fold the empty dough over the filling, aligning the edges and seal the dough around each mound of filling, pressing out any air pockets with your fingertips. Cut the dough between each mound of filling into individual ravioli and press the edges to seal.

Place on parchment lined trays that are lightly floured and do not let the ravioli touch.

Cooking Ravioli
Bring a large pot of water to a boil and add salt. Once water is boiling, add the ravioli and stir. Cook for 2-3 minutes. The ravioli will float to the top. Press them down as they pop up to the top. Drain in a colander and place in serving dish. Add tomato sauce and stir to coat. Serve with additional parmesan cheese.

Penne Alla Vodka Sauce

1 pound penne pasta

1 tablespoon unsalted butter

1 small shallot, minced

1 clove garlic, minced

¼ teaspoon red pepper flakes

½ cup vodka

4 cups of prepared marinara
   sauce (see page 48)

⅔ cup heavy cream

½ cup freshly grated parmesan
   cheese, plus more for topping

Serves 8

Bring a large pot of salted water to a boil. Add the penne and cook as the label directs. Reserve ½ cup cooking water, then drain the pasta.

Meanwhile, melt the butter in a large skillet over medium heat. Add the shallots and cook, stirring occasionally, until slightly softened, about 3 minutes. Add the garlic and red pepper flakes and cook, stirring, 30 seconds.

Remove from the heat and stir in the vodka, marinara sauce and salt/pepper to taste. Return the skillet to medium heat and simmer, stirring often, until the alcohol cooks off, about 7 minutes. Stir in the heavy cream and cook until the sauce thickens slightly, about 3 minutes. Stir in the parmesan cheese.

Add the pasta to the sauce and toss to combine, adding some of the reserved cooking water to loosen, if needed. Season with salt and pepper.

Garnish with more parmesan cheese.

Lasagna Nonna's Way

1 ½ pounds fresh pasta dough

8 ½ cups tomato sauce

1 pound shredded provolone/ mozzarella cheese mix plus an extra cup for the top

8 ounces grated parmesan cheese

Serves 12

Fresh Pasta Dough

1 and ½ pounds fresh pasta (see "Fresh Pasta" recipe, page 42-43) Cut the fresh pasta dough into 6 pieces. Roll out to #6 with a pasta machine and cut sheets to fit into a 9"x13"x2" glass pan. 14 sheets are needed for the 7 layers.

Tomato Sauce

8 ½ cups tomato sauce (see "Tomato Sauce With Meat" recipe, page 49)

Cooking Pasta

Drop 4 sheets of fresh pasta into boiling water and remove after 20 seconds to an ice bath to stop the cooking process. Remove from water and drain in a colandar.

Assembly of Lasagna

Preheat oven to 350 degrees. Spray a 9"x13"x2" glass dish with vegetable spray. Spread ½ cup of sauce on the bottom. Spread out 2 pasta sheets to cover the bottom of the pan. Spread ¾ cup sauce, scant ½ cup provolone/ mozzarella cheese mix and 1 tablespoon grated parmesan cheese.

Continue to repeat until you have about 7 layers of noodles, sauce and cheese. With the last layer of pasta, place 1 cup of sauce on top with the extra 1 cup of cheese.

Bake in the middle of the oven at 350 degrees for 30 minutes or until cheese is melted in the middle. Remove from oven and let rest for 15 minutes before cutting and serving. If you refrigerate, allow 45 minutes to heat up.

Lasagna Bolognese

Ragu:

4 tablespoons extra-virgin olive oil

4 tablespoons butter

¼ pound pancetta, chopped

1 carrot, finely, diced

1 medium onion, diced

1 rib celery, finely diced

¾ pound chuck or veal, ground

¾ pound pork, ground

2 large cloves garlic, finely minced

6 ounces tomato paste

12 ounces beef broth

1 ½ cups dry red wine

Kosher salt and freshly ground
  black pepper

Bechamel Sauce:

6 tablespoons butter

5 tablespoons all-purpose flour

5 cups whole milk

½ teaspoon Kosher salt

¼ teaspoon freshly ground white
  pepper

¼ teaspoon freshly grated nutmeg

1 pound Fresh Spinach Pasta

(page 44)

Ragu

In a 6 to 8-quart, heavy-bottomed saucepan, heat the olive oil and butter over medium heat. Add the carrots, onions, celery and pancetta and sweat over medium heat until the vegetables are translucent and soft but not browned, about 5-7 minutes. Add the garlic, chuck/veal and pork. Continue to stir meat into vegetables and brown the meat. Season meat with salt and pepper. Add the tomato paste, beef broth and wine and bring to a boil and reduce to medium-low heat for 45-60 minutes or until liquid is almost evaporated. Continue to stir frequently so bottom does not burn. Remove from heat.

Add 1 cup béchamel sauce (see recipe below) and mix into the meat sauce.

Béchamel Sauce

In a saucepan, melt the butter and add the flour and cook, stirring with a wooden spoon, to make a light roux, about 2-3 minutes. Whisking constantly, slowly add the milk and continue to cook, stirring occasionally until thickened, 5 minutes. Add the salt, pepper, nutmeg. Place a piece of plastic wrap directly on the surface of the bechamel sauce until ready to assemble the lasagna.

Assembly:

4 ounces parmesan, (2 cups grated)

Prepared béchamel sauce (4 cups)

Prepared ragu sauce (5 cups)

Serves 12

Assembly of Fresh Spinach Pasta

Cut the freesh pasta dough into 5 pieces. Take out one piece and leave the rest covered in plastic. Flatten the piece and coat the entire piece with flour before rolling through the widest setting (#1) on the pasta machine. Roll out the piece of dough to the thinnest setting (#6). Cut into sheets about 12 inches. Place on sheets of floured parchment paper.

Cooking Pasta

Bring about 6 quarts of water to a boil and add 2 tablespoons salt. Set up an ice bath next to the stove top. Drop the pasta sheets into boiling water. Cook about 20 seconds. Drain well and refresh in the ice bath. Drain on towels and set aside.

Assembly of Lasagna

Preheat the oven to 375 degrees. In a 9"x13"x2" glass pan sprayed with vegetable spray, assemble the lasagna, beginning with about 1 cup of ragu, ⅓ cup of grated Parmigiano, a layer of spinach pasta, ½ cup of bechamel, a layer of ragu, a sprinkling of grated parmesan, etc. until all sauce and pasta are used up. The top layer should be pasta with bechamel over it.

Top the lasagna with grated paramesan and bake in the oven for 30 to 45 minutes, until the edges are browned and the sauces are bubbling. Remove and allow to rest for 15 minutes before slicing.

Vegetable Lasagna

1 Pound Fresh Pasta (page 42) or Spinach Pasta (page 44)

Béchamel Sauce:

4 tablespoons butter

4 tablespoons flour

4 cups whole milk

½ teaspoon salt

¼ teaspoon white pepper

⅛ teaspoon fresh grated nutmeg

2 large egg yolks

½ cup heavy cream

Mushroom Layer:

3 tablespoons olive oil

1 pound crimini mushrooms, sliced

1 clove garlic, finely minced

2 tablespoons olive oil

½ pound mixed mushrooms, sliced

½ teaspoon Kosher salt

½ teaspoon fresh ground pepper

2 teaspoons fresh thyme leaves

Dough

Cut the fresh pasta dough into 4 pieces. Roll out to #6 on the pasta machine and cut sheets to fit into a 9" x 13" pan. Eight sheets are needed for the four layers. You will have a few extra pieces.

Béchamel Sauce

Melt butter in a saucepan, add the flour and cook gently 1-2 minutes, stirring constantly. Do not brown. Add the milk and whisk to a smooth consistency. Add salt, pepper and nutmeg; continue cooking and stirring until the sauce thickens. Mix the egg yolks with the heavy cream and add a ladle of hot milk. Whisk egg and cream mixture into saucepan and reheat gently. Do not boil.

Make ahead: Press plastic wrap directly on to the surface to prevent a skin from forming. This sauce will thicken as it stands. Reheat gently before serving, whisking in a little more milk until smooth.

Mushroom Layer

Heat olive oil in large fry pan and cook the crimini mushrooms until golden and any liquid has evaporated. Add the garlic and stir for 30 seconds. Remove from pan and add the 2 tablespoons olive oil and repeat the same with the mixed mushrooms. Remove and mix both mushrooms together and add salt, pepper and thyme. Allow to cool.

Zucchini Layer:

3 tablespoons olive oil

1 medium onion, chopped (about 1 ½ cups)

1 ½ pounds (approx. 6 small) zucchini; sliced lengthwise into 3 pieces

1 tablespoons olive oil

Spinach Layer:

2 tablespoons olive oil

1 large shallot, finely minced

1 clove garlic, finely minced

1 pound fresh baby spinach

Cheese:

8 ounces asiago fresco cheese, shredded (about 2 ¼ cups)

2 ounces parmesan cheese, grated (about 1 cup)

Serves 12

Zucchini Layer

Heat oil in a large fry pan and cook onion until they start to caramelize. Place zucchini cut side down in pan and cook for 1 minute. Remove from heat and cool.

Spinach Layer

Heat oil, shallot and garlic in a large fry pan and add spinach in batches as it wilts and cooks. Keep stirring until the entire amount is wilted. Cool and season with salt and pepper.

Cheese

Mix these cheeses together.

Assembly

Bring a pot of water to a boil and add a few tablespoons of salt. Drop 4 pieces of pasta into the water and cook about 20 seconds, stirring. Scoop out the pasta with a large strainer and place in a bowl of ice water to stop the cooking. Remove pasta and spread it on kitchen towels. Pat dry with another towel. Repeat with the remaining 4 pieces.

Spray the bottom of the 9"x13"x2" glass dish with nonstick cooking spray. Using a rubber spatula, evenly distribute 1 cup béchamel sauce in bottom of the baking dish. Place 2 sheets of pasta in bottom of pan. Spread ¾ cup sauce evenly over noodles followed by the layer of zucchini/onion mixture as well as ¾ cup cheese. Another layer of noodles, sauce, mushroom mixture and cheese. Another layer of noodles, sauce, spinach and cheese. Place remaining noodles on top of last layer. Spread remaining sauce over noodles and sprinkle with remaining cheese. Lightly spray foil with nonstick cooking spray and cover lasagna. Bake in a 425 degree oven until bubbling, about 20 minutes. Cool 15 minutes before cutting and serving.

Cannelloni with Ricotta & Spinach

Filling:

1 box (10 ounce) frozen chopped spinach, thawed and excess liquid squeezed out

1 small shallot, minced

15 ounces whole milk ricotta (page 175)

1 cup freshly grated parmesan

2 large eggs

Pinch of kosher salt

Freshly ground black pepper

½ Pound Fresh Pasta (page 42)

Simple Tomato Sauce:

¼ cup olive oil

½ cup onion, finely minced (1 small onion)

2 garlic cloves, minced

(26-32 ounce) strained tomatoes or crushed tomatoes

1 teaspoon pesto (page 111)

1 package (¾ ounce) fresh basil leaves only, thinly sliced

½ tsp Kosher salt

Freshly ground pepper

Filling
Mix all ingredients together and refrigerate.

Fresh Pasta
Prepare ½ pound fresh pasta dough recipe on page 42-43.

Simple Tomato Sauce
Heat oil and add onion. Sauté for 3-5 minutes. Add garlic and stir for 1 minute. Add the tomatoes, pesto, basil, salt, and pepper. Cook, uncovered on medium heat for 8-10 minutes, stirring occasionally.

Assembly
Take the rested pasta dough and cut in half. Rewrap the other piece in the plastic wrap so it will not dry out. Place parchment paper on trays. Also, have flour for sprinkling and a pizza cutter.

Rolling out the pasta dough
Sprinkle flour generously on both sides of pasta. Attach the pasta machine to the work surface. Turn the knob to the widest setting (usually #1). Press the first piece of dough with your hands into a small rectangle and roll it through the machine. Follow the rolling fresh pasta instructions and roll out thin to #6 depending on the pasta machine. Cut the long, flattened piece of dough into six pieces approximately 4x6-inches. Lay the individual pieces flat on the prepared trays. Roll out the remaining dough following the same instructions.

Topping:

6-7 slices of provolone cheese

2 ounces parmesan, grated

Serves 6

Bring a large pot of water to a boil and add a few tablespoons of salt. Drop 3 pieces of pasta into the water and cook about 15 seconds, stirring. Scoop out the pasta with a large strainer and place in a large bowl of very cold water to stop the cooking. Remove the pasta immediately and spread it on kitchen towels. Pat dry with another towel. Cook all pasta pieces in this manner.

Assembly

Lay the pasta on a work surface and place 2 tablespoons of the filling down the center of each rectangle. Roll up the pasta over the filling to make a tube. Repeat with the remaining 11 pieces.

Preheat the oven to 400 degrees.

Spray a 9"x13"x2" pan with vegetable spray and then evenly spread the bottom of pan with 1 cup of tomato sauce. Place cannelloni (seam side down) into the bottom of the pan. Place them close together, almost overlapping so that all 12 fit in one layer on the bottom.

Pour the remaining tomato sauce over all of the cannelloni. Top with slices of provolone. Bake until the cheese is melted and the cannelloni are lightly golden, 15-25 minutes. Serve with a little grated parmesan cheese on top.

Linguine with Tuna Fish

½ cup olive oil

1 large onion, diced

2 cloves garlic, minced

¾ cup dry white wine

1 can (28 ounces) whole peeled
    tomatoes, hand crushed

½ red pepper

1 tablespoon pesto (page 111)

½ package fresh basil

1 jar (6.7 ounces) white tuna
    fillets in olive oil

(26-32 ounce) strained tomatoes
    or crushed tomatoes

½ pkg. basil leaves only, sliced
    thin like ribbons

2 pounds linguine pasta

Garnish with grated parmesan
    cheese

½ package basil leaves, stacked,
    rolled and thinly sliced

Serves 12-15

In an 6 quart saucepan, heat the olive oil and sauté the onion until transparent. Add the garlic and wine and reduce until the wine evaporates. Add the can of crushed whole tomatoes, ½ red pepper, pesto, ½ package of whole basil and the whole jar of tuna with the oil. On high heat bring the tomatoes to a boil. Then reduce the heat to low so it continues to softly bubble, about 30 minutes. Don't forget to stir so the bottom will not burn.

Add the crushed tomatoes and bring back to a slow boil. Stir occasionally. Let it cook for another 45 minutes to one hour. Add the basil leaves that you have cut like ribbons to the sauce just before serving.

Serve with 2 pounds of linguine cooked according to package directions.

Ricotta Gnocchi

3 cups all-purpose flour

1 cup fresh grated parmesan
cheese

**1 pound whole milk ricotta
(page 175) drained 2 hours**

1 large egg, lightly beaten

½ teaspoon salt

Serves 6

Put the flour into a bowl, make a well in the flour, and add the parmesan cheese, egg and salt. Begin to press together and knead with your hands. Remove dough from the mixing bowl when you have a ball of dough that is soft but not sticky. On a lightly floured surface, knead the dough until it is smooth, about 2 minutes. Let the dough rest uncovered at room temperature for 15 minutes.

Cut off pieces the size of an egg. On a lightly floured surface, roll the dough into a rope ¼ inch in diameter. With a knife, cut the rope into ½ inch pieces. With your index and third fingers held together, gently press down on each piece, beginning at the top and moving down toward the bottom, dragging your fingers toward you and causing the pasta to roll over on itself. You can also roll each gnocchi on the tines of a fork or a gnocchi board with lines. Transfer the formed gnocchi to a tray lined with parchment paper (lightly floured) and make sure that they are not touching each other.

Cooking Gnocchi
Bring a large pan of salted water to a boil, and add the gnocchi. Stir the gnocchi in the water so they don't stick to the bottom of the pan. Cook until the gnocchi are softened, 4-5 minutes or until they all float to the top. Continue to press down and stir. Drain and toss with your favorite sauce.

To freeze leftover gnocchi, place the tray of gnocchi in the freezer. When they have frozen, place in a zip-lock bag and mark with the date. Store no longer than 2 months.

Potato Gnocchi

2 medium-large size russet potatoes (2 cups riced/mashed
potatoes)

1 cup unbleached all-purpose
flour

½ teaspoon salt

1 large egg

Serves 3-4

Wash/scrub the potatoes but do not peel them. Place the potatoes in a large pot and cover with cold water. Bring to a boil over high heat and cook potatoes until tender, about 40 minutes. Test for doneness by piercing a potato with a fork. If the fork enters easily, the potatoes are done. Drain and cool the potatoes. Once cool enough to handle, cut potatoes in half.

Place the flour and salt in a medium bowl. Pass the potatoes (cut side down) through a ricer directly in the bowl on top of the flour. Remove the potato skin. Repeat with remaining potato. Place the egg on top.

With a spatula, cut the potatoes into the flour. Work the dough by cutting, pressing, and turning it over on itself with the spatula. Finish by squeezing the clumps together to form a ball of dough. Keep working until the dough comes together and is soft, pliable, and just a bit sticky. Do not overwork or you will have to add more flour.

Turn out the dough onto a cutting board. With a knife, cut off a piece the size of an egg and roll into ropes about ½-inch in diameter, cutting them in half if they're too long to work with. You will need to add a little more flour to the working surface if it is sticking when you roll them. Cut the ropes into nuggets that are approximately 1-inch long.

Curl each piece by pressing lightly with your index and middle fingers and pulling your finger along the piece of dough toward you. Gnocchi may also be shaped by pressing each piece lightly with a floured fork to form an indentation.

Transfer the gnocchi to a well-floured linen towel on a sheet pan. Do not place on top of each other. Spread them out evenly on the towel. They can be cooked immediately or be kept in the refrigerator for a few hours, until ready to cook.

Cooking Gnocchi

Bring a large pot of salted water to a boil and add the gnocchi. Let them cook for about 5 minutes, or until they all float. Drain and toss with your favorite sauce.

Note: If the gnocchi are not going to be cooked right away, they should be frozen. They can be made up to two weeks in advance. To freeze, lay gnocchi in one layer on sheet pans and put in freezer. Once they are frozen solid they can be transferred to sealable bags or wrapped tightly to avoid freezer burn. Do not thaw them before cooking or they will stick together. To cook them, throw the frozen gnocchi directly into the boiling salted water. The cooking time will be slightly longer until they all float than for unfrozen gnocchi but the preparation should be completed in the same manner as with fresh gnocchi.

Spinach & Potato Gnocchi

1 medium-large size Russet potato (1 cup riced/mashed potatoes)

½ teaspoon salt

¼ teaspoon black pepper

⅛ teaspoon fresh grated nutmeg

1 cup unbleached all-purpose flour, plus extra as needed

¼ cup parmesan cheese, grated

1 large egg

1 (10 ounces) box of frozen spinach, thawed and squeeze excess moisture

½ cup whole milk ricotta (page 175) drained 2 hours

Preheat oven to 400 degrees. Wash and insert a knife into the potato skin three times. Place directly on the oven rack and roast until tender, about one hour or until a knife inserts easily. Remove from oven and cut in half so that steam can escape and not be trapped. When it is cool enough to handle, peel off the skin and remove any dark spots.

Use a potato ricer, masher or fork to mash the potato finely while still warm onto parchment paper. Add salt, pepper, nutmeg, flour and cheese on top.

In a food processor blend egg and spinach for 20 seconds. Add ricotta and blend for 10 seconds.

Add spinach mixture to potato and with a spatula, cut the flour into the potatoes. Work the dough by cutting, pressing, and turning it over on itself with the spatula. Finish by squeezing the clumps together to form a ball of dough. Keep working until the dough comes together and is soft, pliable, and just a bit sticky. Do not overwork or the dough will be too sticky and you will have to add more flour which will make the gnocchi heavy.

Turn out the dough onto a cutting board. With a knife, cut off a piece the size of an egg and roll into ropes about ½-inch in diameter, cutting them in half if they're too long to work with. You will need to add a little more flour to the working surface if it is sticking when you roll them. Cut the ropes into nuggets that are 1-inch long.

Curl each piece by pressing lightly with your index and middle fingers and pulling your finger along the piece of dough toward you. Gnocchi may also be shaped by pressing each piece lightly with a floured fork to form an indentation.

Tomato Cream Sauce:

¼ cup extra-virgin olive oil

1 medium onion, chopped

1 large clove garlic, finely
   minced

1 box (29-32) ounce) strained or
   crushed tomatoes

1 teaspoon pesto (page 111)

¼ cup fresh basil, chiffonade

   Fresh ground pepper

Pinch of Kosher salt

⅔ cup heavy cream

   Garnish with grated Parmesan
   cheese

Serves 3-4

Transfer the gnocchi to a well-floured linen towel on a sheet pan. Do not place on top of each other. Spread them out evenly on the towel. They can be cooked immediately or be kept in the refrigerator for a few hours, until ready to cook.

Cooking Gnocchi

Bring a large pot of salted water to a boil and add the gnocchi. Let them cook for about 5 minutes, or until they all float. Drain and toss with your favorite sauce.

Note: If the gnocchi are not to be cooked right away, they should be frozen. They can be made up to two weeks in advance. To freeze, lay gnocchi in one layer on sheet pans and put in freezer. Once they are frozen solid they can be transferred to sealable bags or wrapped tightly to avoid freezer burn. Do not thaw them before cooking or they will stick together. To cook them, throw the frozen gnocchi directly into the boiling salted water. The cooking time will be slightly longer than for unfrozen gnocchi but the preparation should be completed in the same manner as with fresh gnocchi.

Tomato Cream Sauce

Heat the olive oil in a saucepan and sauté the onion until softened, about 4-5 minutes. Add garlic and stir for 30 seconds and then pour in the tomatoes. Add the pesto, basil, salt and pepper. Simmer gently for 12-15 minutes. Whisk in the heavy cream, and heat—don't bring to a boil. Serve over spinach gnocchi. Garnish with grated Parmesan cheese.

Sweet Potato Gnocchi

1 ½ pounds sweet potatoes (about 2 cups)

1 cup all-purpose flour, plus additional as needed

1 teaspoon Kosher salt

¼ teaspoon white pepper

¼ teaspoon nutmeg, freshly grated

Serves 3-4

Preheat oven to 400 degrees. Wash and insert a knife into the sweet potato skin three times. Place them on a cookie sheet and roast until tender, about one hour or until a knife inserts easily. Remove from oven and cut in half so that steam can escape and not be trapped. When it is cool enough to handle, peel off the skin and remove any dark spots. Use a fork to mash the potato while still warm.

On parchment paper, place the flour, salt, pepper and nutmeg. Place the mashed potatoes on top of flour.

With a spatula, cut the flour into the potatoes. Work the dough by cutting, pressing, and turning it over on itself with the spatula. Finish by squeezing the clumps together to form a ball of dough. Keep working until the dough comes together and is soft, pliable, and just a bit sticky. Do not overwork or the dough will be too sticky and you will have to add more flour which will make the gnocchi heavy.

Turn out the dough onto a cutting board. With a knife, cut off a piece the size of an egg and roll into ropes about ½-inch in diameter, cutting them in half if they're too long to work with. You will need to add a little more flour to the working surface if it is sticking when you roll them. Cut the ropes into nuggets that are approximately 1-inch long.

Curl each piece by pressing lightly with your index and middle fingers and pulling your finger along the piece of dough toward you. Gnocchi may also be shaped by pressing each piece lightly with a floured fork to form an indentation.

Transfer the gnocchi to a well-floured parchment paper on a sheet pan. Do not place on top of each other. Spread them out evenly on the prepared pan. They can be cooked immediately or be kept in the refrigerator for a few hours, until ready to cook.

Cooking Gnocchi

Bring a large pot of salted water to a boil and add the gnocchi. Let them cook for about 5 minutes, or until they all float. Drain and toss with your favorite sauce.

Note: If the gnocchi are not to be cooked right away, they should be frozen. They can be made up to two weeks in advance. To freeze, lay gnocchi in one layer on sheet pans and put in freezer. Once they are frozen solid they can be transferred to sealable bags or wrapped tightly to avoid freezer burn. Do not thaw them before cooking or they will stick together. To cook them, throw the frozen gnocchi directly into the boiling salted water. The cooking time will be slightly longer than for unfrozen gnocchi but the preparation should be completed in the same manner as with fresh gnocchi.

Recommended Sauces: Brown Butter & Sage (see page 64) or Four Cheese Sauce (see page 84).

Four Cheese Sauce

1 tablespoon butter

½ cup heavy cream

¾ cup shredded provolone
cheese (3 ounces)

1 cup parmesan cheese, grated
(4 ounces)

¾ cup shredded asiago fresco
(3 ounces)

4 ounces mascarpone cheese

Fresh ground white pepper

Serves 6

For the gnocchi: double the gnocchi recipe (about 160-200)

Heat butter and heavy cream over low heat. Add cheeses and stir until melted and well combined 2-3 minutes. Add salt and white pepper to taste. Remove from heat and cover to keep warm. Pour over gnocchi and stir to coat.

Macaroni & Cheese

1 pound elbow macaroni, small shells or cavatappi pasta

5 tablespoons butter

5 tablespoons all-purpose flour

4 cups whole milk

12 ounces sharp cheddar cheese, shredded (3 cups)

Salt and pepper

⅔ cup plain bread crumbs or panko bread crumbs

2 tablespoons parmesan cheese, grated

2 tablespoons butter, melted

Serves 12

Preheat oven to 350 degrees.

Cook the macaroni in boiling water for only 5 minutes. (The macaroni will still be hard.) Drain and pour into a 9"x13"x2" glass dish that has been coated with vegetable spray.

While the water is heating up, melt the butter in a sauce pan. Add flour and whisk together over medium-high heat. Cook for 2 minutes whisking constantly.

Pour in the milk and whisk until smooth. Reduce heat to medium-low. Add the cheese and stir to melt. Add a pinch of salt and pepper. Remove from heat once cheese has melted.

Pour the finished cheese sauce over the pasta and into the prepared pan. Stir to combine with pasta.

Mix the bread crumbs with the parmesan cheese and melted butter and sprinkle on top of macaroni.

Bake until bubbly and golden on top, about 10 minutes.

Polenta with Pork Ragu

Polenta:

10 cups water (or milk)

2 teaspoons salt

2 cups polenta, fine grind (not quick-cooking)

4 tablespoons unsalted butter

2 tablespoons extra-virgin olive oil

Whole milk, as needed (approximately a cup)

Sauce:

2 pounds of pork meat (Boston Butt), coarsely ground

2 cloves garlic, finely minced

1 tablespoon pesto (page 111)

1 ½ teaspoons Kosher salt

¾ teaspoon freshly ground pepper

2 teaspoons dried rosemary, ground

1 tablespoon dried fennel, ground

1 teaspoon dried sage, ground

4 tablespoons olive oil, divided

Polenta

Bring water and salt to a boil over high heat in a 4-quart heavy pot, then add polenta in a slow stream, whisking. Cook over medium heat, whisking 2 minutes. Polenta will begin to thicken. Reduce heat to low and cook at a bare simmer, uncovered, stirring frequently with a long-handled spoon.

If it seems to be getting too thick, splash a little milk on top and stir it in—do this occasionally, or as needed. Polenta pops like lava when boiling, so be careful! The cornmeal becomes polenta in 35-45 minutes, when it forms a mass that pulls cleanly away from the sides of the pot. You are looking for a lush, corn flavor and a texture that's smooth, not grainy.

Now add salt and pepper to taste, and another splash of milk, and stir well. Remove from heat, then add butter and olive oil and stir until incorporated.

To serve soft polenta, pour into a large oval platter for serving at the table.

Sauce

Mix ground pork with garlic, pesto, salt, pepper and the dried spices so the spices are evenly distributed.

Heat 2 tablespoons of olive oil in a dutch oven and place half of the pork meat in the pan. Cook until no longer pink and pork has browned up. Remove all of the cooked pork to another dish. Repeat with 2 tablespoons of olive oil and fry the remaining pork in the same manner. Remove the cooked pork.

⅓ cup extra virgin olive oil

1 medium onion, chopped

6 small mini carrots, shredded

3 cloves garlic, finely minced

1 cup red wine

1 can (28 ounce) whole peeled
   tomatoes (hand crush)

1 can (14 ounces) chicken broth

1 tablespoon pesto (page 111)

1 red pepper, cut in half

1 package (¾ oz) fresh basil
   (reserve 1 stem with leaves
   attached)

2 (26-32 ounce) strained tomatoes or crushed tomatoes

Kosher salt and freshly ground
   pepper, to taste

Serves 8

Heat the olive oil in the same pan dutch oven and add onion and carrot; cook for about 5 minutes or until onion is transparent. Add garlic and wine and return the cooked pork meat back into the dutch oven and allow the wine to completely reduce.

Pour in crushed tomatoes, chicken broth, pesto and red pepper. Add ½ package of basil, reserving the one stem for later. Continue cooking and stirring on medium heat for 30 minutes.

Once tomatoes have broken down, add the 2 boxes of strained tomatoes. Cook on low-medium heat for 45 minutes. Continue to stir to prevent scorching on the bottom of the pan.

Take reserved basil stem and remove all the leaves. Stack the leaves on top of each other and cut thin ribbons of basil and add to the sauce. Don't forget to remove the cooked basil stems and the red pepper.

Serve pork ragu over polenta and topped with freshly grated parmesan cheese.

Homemade Cavatelli

4 cups all-purpose flour

1 large egg

2 cups whole milk ricotta (page 175) drained 2 hours

1 teaspoon salt

1 cup grated parmesan cheese

¼ cup half and half

Yields 1 pound of cavatelli

Place your flour in a bowl and make a well in the center. Add your other ingredients into the well and stir until the dough comes together. Dump the dough onto a floured surface and knead with your hands for 2 to 3 minutes until smooth. Cover with plastic wrap and let the dough rest for 15 minutes. You may also wrap the dough in plastic and refrigerate it until needed. This rest period is necessary to obtain the right texture of the dough.

To form the cavatelli by machine

When ready to cut the cavatelli, cut off a piece of dough about the size of a walnut. Roll the dough into a long snake on a lightly floured surface. Flatten the snake so that it will fit through the rollers. (Make sure that it is not wider than the rollers so it will be able to pass through the rollers.) Flour the strip well, and using one hand, pass it through the wooden rollers, turning the crank clockwise with the other hand. The cavatelli will drop onto the counter after they are cut. Place the cavatelli on a lightly floured baking sheet lined with parchment paper and refrigerate until ready to cook.

To form the cavatelli by hand

Working with one piece of dough about the size of a walnut (cover the remaining dough with an inverted bowl to keep the dough from drying out), on a lightly floured surface, roll the dough into a rope ¼ inch in diameter. With a knife, cut the rope into ½-inch pieces. With your index and third fingers held together, gently press down on each piece, beginning at the top and moving down toward the bottom, dragging your fingers toward you and causing the pasta to roll over on itself. Transfer the formed pasta to a lightly floured baking sheet lined with parchment paper and make sure they are not touching or on top of each other.

Another method by hand

Roll the dough into a ½" thick rope working from the center to the edges to maintain an even thickness as you go. Cut the rope into ¼" pieces. Using the tines of a fork, press the cavatelli down and push away so that each piece has groves.

Cooking Cavatelli

Cook cavatelli in a large pot of boiling salted water for about 5 minutes. Like gnocchi, cavatelli will rise to the surface when cooked. Drain and top with a sauce of your choice.

Cavatelli with Sausage & Broccoli

Part One:

1 pound of Italian sausage, casings removed

2 tablespoons olive oil

2 tablespoons butter

1 medium onion, sliced

1 clove garlic, finely minced

¼ cup fresh flat leaf parsley, finely minced

Part Two:

2 tablespoons olive oil

2 cloves garlic, cut in half

2 crowns of broccoli, rinsed and cut into 2-inch pieces

⅓ cup of chicken broth

Freshly ground pepper

Serves 8

This recipe requires 1 pound homemade cavatelli (see "Homemade Cavatelli" on page 86-87).

Part One
In a large skillet over medium-high heat, break up sausage with a wooden spoon. Cook the sausage until no longer pink. Remove from pan and set aside.

In same skillet add the olive oil and butter and sauté the onion until the onions turn translucent, about 5 minutes. Add garlic and stir for 30 seconds. Remove from heat and add parsley. Add this to the cooked sausage.

Part Two
Heat oil and sliced garlic on high in a pan. Once garlic is light and golden, add the broccoli, chicken broth and fresh ground pepper. Cover with a lid and let it steam, about 5 minutes. Uncover when water is evaporated and broccoli is tender. Add to the sausage and onions.

Cook cavatelli in a large pot of boiling salted water for about 5 minutes. Like gnocchi, cavatelli will rise to the surface when cooked. Drain the pasta and pour into a serving dish. Add all of the sausage, onion and broccoli and toss to combine.

Garnish with freshly grated parmesan cheese.

Angel Hair Pasta

1 pound angel hair pasta

⅔ cup extra virgin olive oil

10 cloves garlic, peeled and
   thinly sliced

Freshly ground black pepper

Kosher salt

Freshly grated parmesan cheese,
   garnish

½ cup flat leaf parsley, chopped

Serves 6-8

Fill a large pot with 4 quarts of water. Bring to a boil and then add salt.

In a fry pan on low-medium heat, add olive oil and sliced garlic. Add 5 grindings of fresh black pepper and a good pinch of kosher salt. Cook garlic just until it is lightly golden in color. Remove from heat and set aside until pasta is cooked.

Add pasta to salted boiling water and cook to package directions. Drain in a colander and pour into the serving dish. Pour hot garlic/olive oil mixture over pasta and toss together so that all pasta is coated with oil.

Top with freshly grated parmesan cheese and parsley.

Baked Ziti

Meat mixture:

½ pound ground chuck

½ pound ground pork

1 tablespoon plain bread crumbs

1 tablespoon milk

1 large egg

⅓ cup grated parmesan cheese

1 medium garlic clove, finely minced

1 tablespoon parsley, finely minced

1 teaspoon Kosher salt

¼ teaspoon black pepper

Tomato Sauce

1/3 cup olive oil

1 medium onion, chopped

1 cup red wine

2 cloves garlic, finely minced

14.5 ounce petite diced tomatoes

28-32 ounces strained or crushed tomatoes

¾ cup chicken broth

1 tablespoon pesto (page 111)

1 package fresh basil, divided

Meat mixture
Gently mix together all of the meat ingredients (do not overmix) and set aside.

Tomato Sauce
In a 6 quart dutch oven cook onion in olive oil on high heat until softened, 5 minutes. Add the meat mixture and brown all of the meat. Add the wine and garlic. Allow wine to completely reduce before adding diced and crushed tomatoes. Add chicken broth, pesto, and 1 stem of fresh basil. Bring to a boil and reduce heat so that mixture continues to simmer. Season with salt and pepper and continue to simmer uncovered for 30 minutes. Stir frequently to prevent scorching.

Discard the cooked basil stem. Remove the leaves from the remaining stem of basil. Stack up the leaves, roll and cut into thin strips and drop into the sauce when it is finished cooking.

Ziti

1 pound ziti pasta

Cheese

4 ounces of provolone cheese, grated (1 cup) Reserve ⅓ cup

4 ounces of mozzarella cheese, grated (1 cup) Reserve ⅓ cup

4 ounces of parmesan cheese, grated (1 cup) Reserve ⅓ cup

(Reserved cheese will be for the top.)

Serves 12

Cooking Ziti

Cook the pasta in salted boiling water until still firm, just 6 minutes. It will finish cooking when it bakes in the oven. Drain pasta and pour into a 9"x13"x2" glass pan.

Assembly

Pour tomato sauce/meat mixture over the pasta and mix together. Add the three cheeses and combine all together. Top with reserved provolone/mozzarella/parmesan cheese.

Cover with foil and bake at 350 degrees for about 20-30 minutes or refrigerate overnight and bake for about 45 minutes or until cheese is melted in the center.

Bow Tie Pasta with Sun Dried Tomatoes & Spinach

⅓ cup extra virgin olive oil

1 extra large onion, cut in half and thinly sliced

1 pound baby bella mushrooms, sliced

2 cloves garlic, finely minced

3.5 ounces sun dried tomatoes, julienne cut

10 ounces fresh baby spinach

1 cup heavy cream

Kosher salt and freshly ground black pepper

1 pound of bow tie pasta

½ cup pine nuts, toasted

Garnish with freshly grated parmesan cheese

Serves 8

While water is heating, pour olive oil in a 12 inch pan and place on high heat. Once oil is hot, add onions and cook until they begin to soften (about 5 minutes). Add mushrooms and continue to stir fry over high heat until mushrooms are golden. Add the garlic, sun dried tomatoes and spinach and stir for a couple of minutes until spinach starts to wilt. Pour in cream and allow cream to bubble. Remove from heat and add salt and pepper to taste. Transfer to a serving dish.

Cook pasta according to package for "al dente" in salted boiling water.

Once pasta is finished cooking, drain the water and pour into the serving dish with the cooked vegetables. Mix all together until incorporated.

Garnish with pine nuts and parmesan cheese.

Bow Tie Pasta with Prosciutto & Peas

½ cup extra virgin olive oil

1 extra large onion, cut in half and thinly sliced

1 pound baby bella mushrooms or crimini mushrooms, sliced

2 cloves garlic, finely minced

½ pound snow peas

¼ pound prosciutto ham, separate slices and tear into small pieces

2 cups frozen peas

1 pound bow tie pasta

Kosher salt and freshly ground black pepper

Garnish with freshly grated parmesan cheese

Serves 8

While water is heating, pour olive oil in a 12 inch sauté pan and place on high heat. Once oil is hot, add onions and cook until they begin to soften (about 5 minutes). Add mushrooms and continue to stir fry over high heat until mushrooms are golden. Add the garlic and the snow peas and stir for 1 minute. Take off heat and add frozen peas and torn prosciutto. Stir to incorporate. Add salt and pepper to taste. Transfer to a serving dish.

Cook pasta according to package directions for "al dente" in salted water.

Once pasta is finished cooking, drain the water and pour pasta into the serving dish with the cooked vegetables. Mix all together until incorporated.

Garnish with grated parmesan cheese.

Fettuccine Alfredo

4 tablespoons butter

2 tablespoons flour

2 cups half and half

1 cup freshly grated parmesan cheese (plus more for top-ping)

1 pound fettuccine, cooked al dente

Garnish: fresh ground pepper, chopped parsley and parme-san cheese

Serves 8

Place butter in a sauce pan and melt over medium heat. Add the flour and cook for a couple of minutes. Add half and half and cheese.

Continue cooking over medium-low heat until thickened. Do NOT bring to boil. Pour over cooked pasta. Toss to coat evenly.

Top with fresh ground pepper, parmesan cheese and chopped parsley.

Bucatini Alla Carbonara

1 tablespoon olive oil

2 tablespoons unsalted butter

4 ounces pancetta, diced

1 medium shallot, finely minced

5 large egg yolks

½ cup heavy cream

½ cup fresh grated parmesan cheese, plus additional for serving

1 pound bucatini pasta

Fresh Italian parsley, minced for garnish

Serves 8

Heat the oil and butter in a pan, then add the pancetta; sauté over medium heat to cook the pancetta. Just before it is brown and the fat has rendered, add the shallot and stir to cook together.

In a bowl mix together the egg yolks, heavy cream and cheese.

Meanwhile, cook the pasta until just "al dente". Drain the pasta and pour into the pan with the pancetta mixture. Toss to coat and pour the egg mixture over the pasta. Toss quickly to coat the strands with the sauce; the eggs will cook with the heat of the pasta. Serve immediately.

Top with additional parmesan cheese and garnish with parsley.

Chicken Porchetta

Meat: Beef, Pork, Poultry & Fish

Mary's Meatballs

Meatballs:

1 cup whole milk ricotta (page 175)

1 pound ground chuck

1 pound ground pork

1 pound ground veal*

1 cup freshly grated parmesan cheese

3 large eggs

¼ cup fresh parsley, minced

3 cloves garlic, finely minced or pressed

1 tablespoon Kosher salt

1 teaspoon fresh ground pepper

To Fry:

2 cups corn oil

Yields 45 meatballs

Meatballs:

Mix ricotta, ground chuck, groud pork, ground veal, parmesan cheese, eggs, parsely, garlic, salt and pepper together in a large bowl, but do not over mix. Use an ice cream scoop to form into 45-50 meatballs.

To Fry:

Heat up the oil in a 12" skillet on medium heat and place about 9-10 meatballs carefully into the oil. Brown on one side and gently turn over with a fork to the other side. Remove with a fork once it has browned Repeat with more meatballs. Once meatball are removed, place directly into the tomato sauce to finish cooking for the final 20 minutes.

To Oven Bake:

Place meatballs on a jelly roll pan with sides. Bake in a 400 degree oven for 13 minutes. Remove from oven. Meatballs will not be fully cooked.

Use a spatula to loosen meatballs from the pan and place meatballs into tomato sauce to cook for 10-15 minutes.

To Freeze:

Meatballs can be placed in a disposable freezer bag and frozen for up to 1 month. Place frozen meatballs into the sauce for about 30 minutes.

*You can have equal portions of ground chuck and ground pork (1 ½ pounds) and omit the ground veal.

Beef Tenderloin

5 pounds beef tenderloin, trim off silverskin

Drizzle of olive oil

Kosher salt, garlic salt and black pepper

Serves 10-12

Preheat oven to 425 degrees. Fold the tail end of the beef under to create a roll of meat that is even in thickness. Tie with butcher's twine to secure This will help it cook evenly. Once it's tied, drizzle a little olive oil on top and rub in. Season the beef generously with salt, garlic salt and pepper on all sides.

Roast meat in a pan with sides for 45-50 minutes or until a meat thermometer inserted in the thickest part of the meat registers 130-135 degrees for medium-rare. Transfer roast to a cutting board and tent with foil. Let rest for 10 minutes before slicing.

Italian Beef Stew

¼ cup olive oil

2 tablespoons butter

3 pound boneless beef chuck roast, cut into 2" pieces

Kosher salt and black pepper

3 carrots, peeled and cut into 1" pieces

2 celery stalks, diced

1 medium onion, diced

2 tablespoons tomato paste

5 cloves garlic, finely minced

¼ cup all-purpose flour

1 (750 ml) bottle red wine

2 ½ cups beef broth

1 bouquet garni (2 bay leaves, 8 parsley stems, 1 rosemary stem and 8 thyme sprigs tied up in cheese cloth)

Heat the oil and butter in a large stock pot over medium-high heat. Working in batches, season the pieces of meat with salt/pepper, brown them and remove them to another dish.

When all of the meat is browned, add the carrots, celery and onions in the same pot, until the vegetables are softened. Add the tomato paste and garlic, and stir for 1 minute. Add the flour and cook, stirring for 2 minutes.

Pour in the entire bottle of wine and the beef broth. Make sure you scrape the bottom of the pan to loosen up all of the bits. Add the bouquet garni. Return the meat to the pot.

Bring the mixture up to a boil and then reduce the heat to a simmer and cook uncovered until the liquid starts to thicken, about 15-20 minutes.

Cover with a lid and cook on low heat for 2 hours. Stir occasionally.

1 tablespoon olive oil

½ pound pancetta or bacon, diced

½ bag (8 ounces) frozen pearl onions, thawed

2 teaspoons sugar

1 pound crimini mushrooms, quartered

8 ounces frozen green peas

Garnish with ¼ cup fresh parsley, chopped

Serves 6

While the meat cooks, prepare remaining vegetables. Heat the olive oil, in the pan and brown the pancetta; remove pancetta and add the onions and sugar to the pan. Cook onions and sugar until browned all over and then remove. Finally brown the mushrooms then remove and set aside.

After the 2 hours, add the cooked pancetta, pearl onions and mushrooms. Turn up the heat slightly and simmer, uncovered, for 30 minutes more, until the meat is tender.

Add the frozen peas during the last minute of cooking.

Season with salt and pepper to taste.

Remove the bouquet garni.

Serve with mashed potatoes or buttered noodles.

Round Steak

Round Steak:

2 pound beef round steak

Kosher salt and black pepper

½ cup all-purpose flour

2 tablespoons corn oil

Sauce:

3 tablespoons butter

1 medium onion, diced

3 tablespoons all-purpose flour

3 cups beef broth, low sodium

Salt and pepper

Serves 5-6

Round Steak

Tenderize round steak by pounding with a meat mallet on both sides. Season with salt and pepper. Cut into 4 pieces.

Dredge pieces in flour on both sides. Heat oil in a deep pan on medium-high. Add the 4 pieces to the hot oil and cook until browned, about 5-6 minutes per side. Remove the meat to a plate.

Sauce

Add 3 tablespoons butter and cook the onion until softened. Add the flour to the pan scraping the bottom with a wooden spoon. Stir the mixture for 2 minutes. Add the beef broth and whisk until smooth. Return the steak to the pan. Bring the liquid to a boil and reduce heat to low. Cover with a lid. Let simmer for 1 hour or until steak is fork tender. Season with salt and pepper to taste.

Serve with wide noodles or mashed potatoes.

Meatloaf

Vegetables:

2 tablespoons butter

2 stalks celery, finely chopped

1 cup onion, finely chopped

1 clove garlic, finely minced

Meatloaf:

1 pound ground chuck

1 pound ground pork

2 large eggs

1 cup plain bread crumbs

1 can (10 ounces) cream of
  mushroom soup

1 teaspoon kosher salt

½ teaspoon black pepper

⅓ cup ketchup

Serves 6

Preheat oven to 375 degrees.

Vegetables

In a skillet over medium heat, melt the butter. Add the celery and onion and cook until softened, about 4 minutes. Add garlic and stir to mix in with the vegetables. Remove from heat. Allow to cool before adding to the meat mixture.

Meatloaf

In a large bowl, add the cooked vegetables, ground chuck, pork, eggs, bread crumbs, mushroom soup, salt and pepper. Stir together until combined.

Place into a 9"x13"x2" glass pan and form into an even loaf. Drizzle ketchup on the top of the meatloaf and bake for 1 hour.

Beef Pot Roast

¼ cup olive oil

2 tablespoons butter

4 pound boneless beef chuck roast

Kosher salt and black pepper

1 cup baby carrots

2 celery stalks, diced

1 large onion, diced

3 cloves garlic, finely minced

1 cup red wine

1 can (15 ounce) petite diced tomatoes

2 cups beef broth

1 bouquet garni (2 bay leaves, 1 rosemary stem and 8 thyme sprigs tied up in cheese cloth)

Gravy:

3 tablespoons cornstarch

3 tablespoons cold water

Serves 8

Preheat the oven to 350 degrees.

Heat the olive oil and butter in a 6 quart stock pot over medium-high heat. Season the roast and brown for 6 minutes on each side then remove it to another dish.

Add the carrots, celery and onions in the same pot, until the onions have softened, about 5 minutes. Add the garlic and stir for 30 seconds.

Deglaze the pan with the wine scraping up the brown bits on the bottom of the pan. Place the meat back into the pan. Bring it to a boil and allow it to reduce for 4 minutes. Add the tomatoes and beef broth and bring it back to a boil. Add the bouquet garni.

Cover with a lid and place in the oven for 3 hours. Check the roast for tenderness with a fork. Carefully remove the meat to a serving platter.

Gravy

Strain the beef broth through a sieve and place in a saucepan. Skim and remove the layer of grease. Bring to a boil. Mix the cornstarch and cold water and pour into the boiling broth. Let boil for 1 minute or until it thickens.

Serve with the beef and mashed potatoes.

Chicken Cutlets

3 pounds boneless chicken
   breasts or chicken tenders

Kosher salt, pepper, garlic salt

2 large eggs

⅓ cup fresh grated parmesan
   cheese

1 tablespoon chopped parsley

¾ cup dry bread crumbs (plain)

1 ½ cups corn oil for frying

Serves 8

Trim off fat from each chicken breast. Cut through the thickness to make thinner fillets, approximately ¼" thick. Cut each breast into 2 or 3 pieces depending on the size. (Chicken tenders do not have to be cut.) Sprinkle with kosher salt, pepper and a light sprinkle of garlic salt.

Beat the eggs lightly and add the cheese and parsley. Add the chicken to the egg/cheese mixture. Stir until chicken is completely coated. Spread bread crumbs on a separate plate. Dip chicken into bread crumbs and coat both sides.

Heat oil in pan and fry cutlets on medium-high until light and golden on each side. Place in a serving dish lined with paper towels to absorb excess oil. Hold in a preheated 180 degree oven until ready to serve. Do not cover.

Chicken Marsala

6 boneless chicken breasts (about 3 pounds) cut in half thru thickness

Kosher salt and fresh ground pepper

3 tablespoons olive oil

2 tablespoons butter

6 slices provolone cheese, cut in half

1 medium shallot, chopped

8 ounces sliced baby bella or crimini mushrooms

1 garlic clove, minced or pressed

½ cup dry marsala wine

2 tablespoons cornstarch

1 can (14 ounces) low sodium chicken broth

1 tablespoon flat leaf parsley, chopped

Serves 8

Season chicken with salt and pepper. Heat olive oil and butter in a large pan over medium-high heat. Add 6 pieces of chicken and cook uncovered for 5-6 minutes per side until chicken is golden brown. Remove chicken to a 9 x 13 glass dish and place a slice of cheese on top. Repeat for the other 6 pieces of chicken.

Once pan is empty, add the shallots and mushrooms and continue to stir until mushrooms are cooked, 2-3 minutes. Add garlic, marsala wine and season with salt/pepper. While wine is reducing, mix cornstarch with cold chicken broth. Continue to cook until wine reduces and no liquid is left.

Pour in chicken broth/cornstarch mixture and continue to cook until sauce thickens. Pour over the top of the chicken in the 9"x13"x2" pan and place foil over the top. Place in a 350 degree oven for 15-20 minutes. Remove foil and garnish with chopped parsley.

Chicken Pot Pie

2 unbaked 9" pie crusts

Filling:

6 tablespoons butter

½ cup onions, chopped

½ cup celery, chopped

½ cup carrots, chopped

1 medium russet potato, peeled and diced

Kosher salt and black pepper

6 tablespoons all-purpose flour

1 (14 ounce) can chicken broth

1 cup whole milk

1 cup frozen peas

2 cups cooked chicken, cubed (or two chicken breasts)

2 tablespoons parsley, minced

1 egg, beaten

Serves 8

Preheat oven to 400 degrees.

In a stock pot on medium-high heat melt the butter and add the onions, celery, carrots and potatoes. Season with salt and pepper and cook for 7 minutes, stirring frequently, until the potato has softened.

Add the flour over the vegetables and cook for 2-3 minutes, stirring constantly. Pour in the chicken broth and milk and bring it to a boil and then turn the heat down to a simmer. Simmer, stirring occasionally, until it begins to thicken, about 10 minutes.

Stir in the peas, chicken and parsley and remove from heat. Let the filling cool to room temperature.

Line a 9" deep pie pan with one of the pie crusts. Pour the filling into the prepared pan. Place the second crust on top of the filling. Carefully roll and press the overlapping crust with the bottom crust, forming a thick edge. Crimp the edges of the pan with a fork and place on a baking sheet lined with foil.

Lightly brush the entire top crust with the beaten egg and cut three 2" slits on top of the crust for venting.

Bake for 30 minutes or until the crust is golden brown. Remove from the oven and cool for 10 minutes before serving.

Chicken Porchetta

2 tablespoons pesto (page 111)

2 cloves garlic, finely minced

2 tablespoons fresh rosemary, finely minced

1/8 teaspoon allspice

1 flat chicken, 3 pounds (backbone. ribs, and thigh bones are removed)

1 pork tenderloin (1 pound) cut in half

4 chicken thighs (boneless and skinless)

Kosher salt

Freshly ground pepper

Butcher twine

1 metal skewer

2 tablespoons olive oil

½ cup dry white wine

Serves 8-10

Mix the pesto, garlic, rosemary and allspice together and spread it on the flat chicken, pork tenderloin and chicken thighs. Sprinkle with a generous amount of kosher salt and freshly ground black pepper on both sides. Lay the flat chicken skin side down and place the two pork pieces on top of the breast of the flat chicken. Place two chicken thighs on top of the pork and the other two on either side of the stack of meat.

Pull up the flat chicken around the stack of meat. You will need to secure both sides of the skin together with a metal skewer. Cut 3-4 pieces of butcher twine to tie up the chicken porchetta and hold it all together. Cut a smaller piece of butcher twine to tie the drumsticks together.

Place the porchetta seam side down in a 9"x13" glass pan. Drizzle the olive oil on top of the roast. Cover tightly with foil and bake in a 400 degree oven for 45 minutes. Remove foil and pour in the white wine. Place back into the oven and turn up the heat to 425 degrees. Bake uncovered for 30-45 minutes.

A meat thermometer placed in the center of the pork should read 145. Check the temperature of the chicken. It should be at 165 degrees. Once the temperatures are reached, remove from the oven and tent with foil. Let rest for at least 30 minutes before slicing. Serve chicken porchetta with pan juices left in the pan.

Note: Ask your local butcher to cut the chicken for you.

Homemade Pesto

½ bunch Italian parsley (leaves only)

1 large package fresh basil (4 ounces, leaves only)

2 garlic cloves, peeled

1 celery heart (only the yellow center 3 inches with leaves)

⅔ cup olive oil plus more, if needed

¼ teaspoon kosher salt

Yields 12 ounces

Place parsley and basil leaves, garlic cloves, celery, salt and half of the oil in the food processor. Process for 15-20 seconds. Stop and scrape down the sides. Finish adding the additional oil through the top feed tube while processing the pesto. Pesto should be a smooth paste. Add a little more oil if needed.

Pour into a few small containers. Do not fill container more than ⅔ full leaving space to cover the top with a thin layer of oil. As you use the pesto, make sure you replace the layer of oil in order to keep the bright green color. Pesto will keep in the refrigerator for a few months.

Chicken Saltimbocca

4 (8 ounce) boneless, skinless chicken breasts (2 pounds)

4 thin slices prosciutto

8-12 large fresh sage leaves

All-purpose flour for dredging

Kosher salt and fresh ground pepper

1 tablespoon extra-virgin olive oil

1 tablespoon unsalted butter

¼ cup dry white wine

2 tablespoons unsalted butter, cold and cubed

Small sage leaves or cut sage leaves (about 1 tablespoon)

Serves 4

With a meat mallet, pound the chicken breasts to ¼-inch thickness. Season each breast with salt and pepper and lay 2-3 sage leaves on ½ of breast. Lay 1 slice prosciutto over the sage leaves and fold in half like a book. Dredge each breast in the flour.

Heat the oil and butter in a large skillet over medium-high heat. Add the chicken to the pan and cook until golden on the first side, about 3 minutes. Turn and cook the other side, about 2 more minutes.

Add the wine to the pan, stirring to bring up the brown bits in the bottom. Let the wine cook down for a few minutes to burn off the alcohol. Add the remaining butter and sage leaves and swirl the pan around. Pour the sauce and the chicken into a serving platter.

Chicken Breasts in Cream Sauce

Chicken:

4 (8 ounce) boneless chicken breasts (slice in half thru thickness) or 8 boneless chicken thighs

2 tablespoons olive oil

1 teaspoon fresh rosemary, finely chopped

1 teaspoon fresh thyme, finely chopped

1 teaspoon fresh parsley, finely chopped

Kosher salt and fresh ground pepper

4 thin slices prosciutto, cut in half

8 thin slices asiago fresco or provolone

Garnish with fresh parsley, chopped

Cream Sauce:

Pan drippings from chicken

2 tablespoons butter

1 shallot, finely minced

1 clove garlic, finely minced

½ cup white wine

1 cup heavy cream

Serves 6

Chicken

Season chicken with salt and pepper. Combine olive oil and fresh herbs in a medium bowl. Place the chicken in the bowl and coat the chicken with the fresh herb mixture.

Place ½ slice of prosciutto and one slice of cheese on one side of the chicken. Fold the other half of chicken over on top.

Place a drizzle of olive oil in a skillet and cook chicken on one side until it is golden brown. Flip over and do the same on the other side. Remove the chicken to a platter. Tent with foil.

Cream Sauce

Add the butter to sauté the shallots scraping up any brown bits. Add the garlic and wine and reduce until only a small amount of liquid remains. Return the chicken to the pan and add the cream and cook for a few minutes so that it thickens.

Top with chopped parsley.

Roast Chicken

9 "x13"x2" glass pan or roaster

Vegtables:

12 large yukon gold potatoes
washed and cut in half

3 carrots, peeled and cut in half

1 tablespoon fresh rosemary,
finely minced

Kosher salt and black pepper

2 tablespoons olive oil

Chicken:

1 (4 pound) whole chicken

Kosher salt and black pepper

2 cloves of garlic, peeled and cut
in half

½ of a small onion, peeled and
cut in half

1 stalk of celery with leaves, cut
into 3 pieces

One 4" stem of fresh rosemary

Drizzle of olive oil

Serves 12

Vegtables
Preheat oven to 425 degrees. Place cut potatoes and
carrots into a medium sized bowl. Season with rosemary,
kosher salt, pepper and olive oil. Stir to coat well. Place in
the bottom of a roasting pan cut side down.

Chicken
Rinse chicken and remove paper with giblets. Pat dry
with paper towels. Place chicken in the roasting pan and
sprinkle salt inside the chicken cavity. Place garlic, onion,
celery, and rosemary inside chicken cavity.

Sprinkle the outside skin with Kosher salt and pepper on
the bottom side first. Flip over and drizzle a little olive
oil on the skin. Massage it to cover the entire top of the
chicken. Sprinkle more Kosher salt and pepper on top.

Place the chicken on top of the layer of vegetables.

Bake uncovered for about 1 hour and 15 minutes. Use a
thermometer to check the temperature in the middle of
the breast. It should register 165 degrees. The dark meat
should register 175 degrees. 18-20 minutes of cooking
time is needed for each pound of chicken. You may have
to allow for more cooking time depending on how big
your chicken is.

Take pan out of the oven, and remove chicken from the
pan to a carving board. Be sure to let it rest for
15 minutes before carving. Remove vegetables to a
serving platter.

Chicken Thighs with Fresh Herbs

2 ½ pounds boneless, skinless chicken thighs

Kosher salt and black pepper

Marinade:

½ cup white wine

½ cup olive oil

1 tablespoon rosemary, finely minced

1 tablespoon thyme, finely minced

1 tablespoon flat leaf parsley, finely minced

2 teaspoons fresh sage leaves, finely minced

2 cloves garlic, finely minced

3 green onions, finely sliced

Cooking Chicken:

1 tablespoon olive oil

⅓ cup white wine

2 tablespoons butter, cold and cubed

Serves 6

Marinade
Season chicken with salt and pepper on both sides.

Open a 1 gallon reclosable plastic bag. Add the wine, olive oil, rosemary, thyme, parsley, sage, garlic and onion. Add the chicken, seal the bag and remove all air. Massage the bag until the chicken is entirely coated. Place in the refrigerator for 1-2 hours.

Cooking Chicken:
Heat olive oil in a large 12" skillet on high heat. Remove chicken pieces one at a time and place the chicken flat in a fry pan on high heat. Allow to cook and brown on one side before flipping over to the other side. Add white wine and allow to completely reduce. Once the wine has evaporated, reduce heat to medium and stir frequently to continue browning both sides of the chicken.

Add the cold butter and swirl around in the pan until melted to finish the sauce.

Chicken Rollatini

Chicken:

6 boneless chicken breasts

Kosher salt, pepper and garlic salt

6 slices of proscuitto

6 slices of provolone cheese

3 large eggs

1 teaspoon fresh parsley, finely minced

¼ cup parmesan cheese

1 cup plain bread crumbs

2 tablespoons olive oil

3 tablespoons butter

Sauce:

1 tablespoon olive oil

1 shallot, finely minced

⅓ cup dry white wine

2 tablespoons cornstarch

¾ cup half and half

¾ cup chicken broth

1 tablespoon fresh parsley, finely minced

Serves 6

Chicken

Preheat oven to 375 degrees. Flatten chicken breasts between plastic wrap with a meat mallet. Season both sides with salt, pepper and lightly with garlic salt. Lay 1 slice of proscuitto and 1 piece of cheese on the flattened breast. Roll up smaller end first and press to hold together. Repeat process for remaining chicken breasts. Mix eggs, parsley and parmesan cheese together. Dip and coat each roll into the egg mixture and then coat completely with bread crumbs.

Heat olive oil and butter in frying pan and place seam side down and cook until golden brown. Carefully flip over to cook the other side until golden brown, about 4 minutes on each side. Once golden, remove and place in a 9"x13"x2" baking dish. Bake for 20-30 minutes or until internal temperature of chicken is 165 degrees. Remove chicken from oven and serve with the sauce.

Sauce

In the same pan the chicken was cooked, remove loose bread crumbs. Add olive oil and shallot and cook until shallots are translucent, about 3 minutes. Stir in the white wine and let it completely reduce.

Blend together cornstarch, half and half and chicken broth. Slowly stir into the pan and continue stirring until sauce thickens and comes to a boil, about 2-3 minutes. Remove from heat and add the fresh parsley.

Serve the sauce with the chicken.

Sticky Chicken

2 pounds chicken tenders or boneless, skinless chicken thighs

Kosher salt, fresh ground pepper

1 tablespoon fresh rosemary, chopped

2 tablespoons olive oil

½ cup white wine

1 clove garlic, finely minced

2 tablespoons butter

Serves 4-5

Season both sides of chicken with salt, pepper and rosemary. On high heat, place olive oil in a large fry pan. Once oil is hot, add chicken and do not move.

Cook for 3 minutes on one side before turning over all the pieces. Immediately add the wine (don't stir) and let the wine completely evaporate. Once it starts to sizzle, stir chicken and reduce the heat to medium-high. The wine will turn the chicken a golden brown.

Continue to stir until the golden color is on both sides. Add the garlic and stir for 30-60 seconds. Add the butter and swirl in the pan until you have a nice sauce. Transfer to a serving dish.

Teriyaki Chicken

⅓ cup reduced sodium soy sauce

1 tablespoon corn oil

2 tablespoons brown sugar

3 green onions, finely sliced (white part and a 2" portion of the green)

2 cloves garlic, finely minced

½ teaspoon black pepper

2 ½ pounds boneless skinless chicken tenders

Serves 6

Combine soy sauce, oil, brown sugar, onions, garlic and pepper for the marinade in a 1 gallon reclosable plastic freezer bag. Massage the bag until the brown sugar is dissolved. Add the chicken, seal the bag and remove all air. Massage the bag until the chicken is entirely coated. Allow to sit in marinade at least one hour or overnight.

These can be grilled (5-7 minutes), cooked in a large fry pan (until golden on both sides), or baked in the oven (425 degrees for 12 minutes). They cook quickly since they are thin.

The internal temperature should register 165 degrees on a meat thermometer.

Serve with jasmine rice.

Pork Loin

1 boneless pork loin roast (about 4 pounds)

Kosher salt and pepper

⅓ cup white wine

⅓ cup olive oil

2 tablespoons fresh rosemary, leaves removed from stems and chopped finely

2 tablespoons fresh flat leaf parsley, leaves only and chopped finely

2 cloves garlic, finely minced

Two gallon reclosable plastic bag

Serves 6

Season pork loin with salt and pepper. Place wine, olive oil, rosemary, parsely and garlic in the plastic bag. Add meat and close top so that no air remains in the bag. Massage the bag so that the marinade covers all of the meat.

Refrigerate for one hour.

Preheat oven to 425 degrees.

Pour the entire bag into a 9"x13"x2" glass dish.

Insert a probe at an angle into the center of the meat and close the door on the wire that is attached to the thermometer.* Set the internal temperature for 145 degrees. Roast for 1 hour 15 minutes or until the meat reaches an internal temperature of 145 degrees. Remove from oven once it reaches the proper temperature. Allow to rest for 15 minutes before carving.

*NOTE: If you do not have a thermometer that can cook in the meat while in the oven, set the timer for 1 hour and check the internal temperature with an instant read thermometer. It needs to register 145 degrees. Cook for an additional 10-15 minutes and check again.

Porchetta

One 6 ½-7 pound bone-in Boston Butt Pork Shoulder Roast (ask butcher to remove bone)

3 tablespoons olive oil

1 tablespoon fresh sage, finely minced

1 tablespoon fresh thyme, finely minced

3 tablespoons fresh rosemary, finely minced

2 tablespoons fresh parsley finely minced

4 cloves garlic, finely minced

Kosher salt and freshly ground black pepper

1 cup dry white wine

Salsa Verde:

1 bunch fresh parsley, leaves removed from stems

3 cloves garlic

1 medium shallot, cut in half

Juice and zest of ½ lemon

1 cup extra virgin olive oil

Serves 12

Preheat oven to 325 degrees.

Combine the olive oil, sage, thyme, rosemary, parsley and garlic to make a loose paste. Cut the sides of the pork so it opens up like a book and lies flat on your cutting board. Rub the herb mixture all over the inside of the pork. Sprinkle generously with kosher salt and freshly ground black pepper. Roll the pork and tie tightly with butcher's twine. Place the roast (fat side up) in a roasting pan. Season the top with Kosher salt and black pepper. Drizzle olive oil lightly over the roast. It needs to be refrigerated from 6-24 hours.

Bake in the oven and roast covered tightly with foil for 3 hours. Remove foil and pour the white wine on top of the roast. Place back in oven uncovered and baste with the wine and juices every hour. Roast for another 2 hours. Total roasting time is about 5 hours.

Remove from the oven, tent with foil and let rest for 20 minutes. Remove the butcher's twine before slicing.

Salsa Verde

Combine parsley, garlic, shallot, lemon juice and zest in a food processor. While processor is running, drizzle oil in to make a smooth sauce. Let it sit for 2 hours for flavors to combine.

Serve the sauce with the porchetta.

Pork Tenderloin Medallions

2 pork tenderloins (one pound each)

Kosher salt, fresh ground pepper

1 tablespoon rosemary, finely minced

2 tablespoons extra-virgin olive oil

½ cup white wine

2 cloves garlic, minced

2 tablespoons butter, cold

Serves 4-6

Cut tenderloin into 1 ½ " thick pieces (approximately 8 pieces per pound). Season both sides of pork with salt, pepper and rosemary. On high heat place oil in a large sauté pan. Once oil is hot, add pork pieces and allow meat to sear on one side without moving for 2 minutes. Use a spatula and flip over each piece.

Immediately add wine and allow it to reduce (do not stir). Once wine has completely evaporated, stir pork pieces and reduce heat to medium-high. The wine will caramelize the meat. Continue to stir and turn over until a golden color is on both sides. Add the garlic and stir for 30-60 seconds. Add the butter and swirl in the pan until you have a nice sauce.

Transfer to a serving dish.

Pulled Pork

6-7 pound pork butt roast

2 tablespoons brown sugar

2 tablespoons Kosher salt

1 tablespoons paprika

1 tablespoon garlic powder

1 tablespoon onion powder

1 tablespoon black pepper

¼ teaspoon cayenne pepper

1 teaspoon dried thyme

1 teaspoon dried oregano

Serves 12

Place pork butt roast in the roasting pan that will go in the oven. Combine all ingredients thoroughly and rub all of it on the pork roast. Place the seasoned pork roast in the pan, fat side up. Cover with aluminum foil and refrigerate overnight.

Preheat oven to 325 degrees. Bake **covered** for 4 hours.

Remove the foil from the roast and continue to bake until the roast is very tender and will pull apart easily with two fork, 2 hours longer. If it is tough to pull apart, continue baking for an additional 30 minutes. Check for tenderness and if it continues to resist, bake 30 minutes more.

Remove the pork from the oven; set aside to cool slightly. Remove any excess fat from the roast and discard. Pull the pork apart with 2 forks and place in the bottom of the pan with the juice. Mix all of the pork with the juices in the bottom of the pan.

Serve on buns with your favorite barbeque sauce and coleslaw.

Pork Stew with Peas

2 pounds boneless pork loin country ribs, cut into 1" cubes

Kosher salt and black pepper

2 tablespoons olive oil

1 medium onion, chopped

2 cloves garlic, finely minced

½ cup dry white wine

1 can (14 ounce) chicken broth

2 cups crushed tomatoes

1 stem of fresh basil

1 teaspoon pesto (page 111)

4 large eggs

1 cup grated parmesan cheese

12 ounce bag frozen green peas

Serves 8

Season pork on both sides with salt and pepper.

Heat olive oil in a 6 quart stock pot. Cook the pork meat until it lightly browns on all sides. Add the onion, garlic and wine. Cook until most of the liquid is evaporated, about 2 minutes.

Mix in the chicken broth, tomato sauce, basil and pesto and bring to a boil. Reduce heat to low so that it is still bubbling. Place a lid on the pan. Let the meat cook for 45-60 minutes, or until the meat is tender.

Mix the eggs and parmesan cheese together. Remove lid and pour over the entire stew. Do not stir. Place lid back on and continue to cook on a simmer for 15 minutes or until the eggs have set and cooked.

Remove lid and stir in the frozen peas.

Serve with crusty bread.

Roast Turkey

1 whole turkey (10-12 pounds) frozen or fresh

Kosher salt and pepper

1 package fresh herbs (poultry pack: rosemary, thyme, sage)

5 cloves of garlic, peeled and cut in half

1 onion, peeled and cut in half

1 stalk of celery, cut in half or thirds

3 tablespoons butter, melted

1 tablespoon dried rosemary

1 tablespoon dried thyme

1 oven bag and tie to fit a 10-12 pound turkey

1 tablespoon flour

Gravy

2 cups of turkey broth

3 tablespoons cornstarch

3 tablespoons **cold** water

Serves 12

NOTE: If the turkey is frozen, you must thaw it in the refrigerator for at least 5-7 days before you are going to cook it.

Remove plastic around the turkey and remove the giblets/neck from the inside or the back side of the turkey. It will be wrapped in paper and needs to be removed and discarded. Rinse the turkey and pat dry with paper towels.

Place turkey on a cutting board and season the bottom side of the turkey with salt and pepper. Sprinkle a generous pinch of salt inside the cavity. Stuff the package of fresh herbs, garlic, onion and celery inside the cavity of the turkey. Brush the entire top of turkey with melted butter. Season generously with salt, pepper, dried rosemary and thyme.

Open the oven bag and place the tablespoon of flour in. Insert turkey into bag and seal with the twist tie that comes with the bag. Cut six 1" holes on the top of the bag and place into the roasting pan. Cook for 2 hours in a 350 degree oven. Remove and allow it to rest for 30 minutes before removing from the bag and carving.

Gravy
Strain 2 cups of broth from the oven bag and heat up in a saucepan. Mix cornstarch and cold water to make a slurry. Whisk into hot broth and let it come to a boil. Remove and serve with turkey.

Turkey Breast

6-7 pound turkey breast

2 tablespoons olive oil

1 large clove garlic, finely minced

1 tablespoon fresh rosemary, minced

1 tablespoon fresh thyme leaves, minced

1 tablespoon fresh sage, minced

Kosher salt, black pepper

¼ cup parmesan cheese, grated

butcher's twine

2 tablespoons olive oil

½ cup white wine

Serves 8

To debone the turkey breast: Start cutting on the rib end and work your way down to the breast, staying close to the bone. Do the same to the other side until the bone
is removed. Keep the breast skin intact without puncturing. Lay the breast on a cutting board with the skin side down. Remove both tenderloins and place in between the two breast halves. Thicker parts may have to be butterflied to keep an even thickness.

Make a paste with the olive oil, garlic, rosemary, thyme and sage. Rub the herb paste into the meat. Season the turkey breast with salt and pepper. Sprinkle the parmesan cheese over the entire breast meat.

Tuck and roll up the breast tightly. Cut 4-5 pieces of butchers twine to wrap around the roast. Lay out the strings and tie securely and trim the excess string. Place in a 9"x13"x2" glass pan. Drizzle the olive oil over the skin and sprinkle with more salt and pepper. Pour the wine in the bottom of the glass pan.

Cover and bake in a 375 degree oven for 90 minutes. Remove foil and turn up the oven to 450 degrees to brown the skin. Return the turkey to the oven and bake **uncovered** for 10-12 minutes. Check the internal temperature in the center of the thickest part of the breast. The temperature should read 160-165 degrees. If not, cook an additional 5-10 minutes and check again.

Remove from the oven and let the meat rest for 10 minutes before slicing.

The pan juices can be served with the turkey breast.

Rabbit

Rabbit:

1 rabbit (2 ½ - 3 pounds), cut into 8 pieces

Kosher salt and pepper

1 Tablespoon fresh rosemary, finely minced

2 tablespoons olive oil

2 tablespoons butter

1 small onion, thinly sliced

2 cloves garlic, finely minced

½ cup dry white wine

1 cup chicken broth, low sodium

Serves 6

Rabbit

Season the rabbit with salt, pepper and rosemary.

Heat olive oil and butter in 6 quart stock pot and brown the rabbit pieces on medium-high heat, 10-15 minutes.

When all of the rabbit is browned well, add the onion and garlic; cook, stirring until the onions soften, about 5 minutes. Add the wine and bring to a boil Cook until most of the liquid is evaporated, about 2-3 minutes. Add the chicken broth and bring it to a boil. Reduce the heat to low and cover with a lid. Cook the rabbit until tender when pierced with a fork, about 30-45 minutes.

Remove the rabbit to a serving platter. Cover to keep warm. Increase the heat to high to reduce the remaining liquid to a sauce. Once thickened, pour over the rabbit and serve.

Baccala (Salted Cod Fish)

1 pound dried salt cod, soaked*

3 tablespoons olive oil

½ cup onion, chopped

½ cup red bell pepper, chopped

2 medium yukon gold potatoes, peeled and sliced

1 clove garlic, finely minced

12 ounces crushed tomato sauce

½ package fresh basil leaves, cut into thin ribbons

Serves 6

*Soak the cod in cold water in the refrigerator at least 3 days before cooking. The water will need to be changed twice daily.

In a large skillet, heat the oil over medium heat. Add the onion, red pepper and potatoes. Stir and cook the vegetables for 5-7 minutes. Add the garlic and tomato sauce. Bring it to a bubbling simmer. Nestle the pieces of cod into the tomato sauce so they are slightly covered. Put a lid on the pan. Cook until the fish is tender, about 10 minutes. Add the fresh basil leaves. Taste for seasoning and add pepper. You may not need to add salt!

Because salted cod looks whiter and feels firmer than fresh fish, to determine doneness, check to see if the fish feels tender when it is cut.

Orange Roughy

Orange Roughy:

2 pounds orange roughy fillets

Kosher salt and black pepper

Sauce:

¼ cup olive oil

1 small onion, finely chopped

½ red bell pepper, finely chopped

1 clove garlic, finely minced

6 ounces crushed tomatoes

1 package (¾ ounce) fresh basil, 1 stem

½ cup white wine

Fresh basil, finely sliced for garnish

Serves 4-6

Orange Roughy

Season fish with salt and pepper.

Sauce

Heat olive oil in frying pan and cook onion and red bell pepper until they have softened. Add garlic, crushed tomaotes, basil and wine. Nestle the fillets into the sauce so they are slightly covered. Bring to a boil and reduce heat to a simmer. Cook for another 5-6 minutes until fish flakes easily with a fork. Remove the cooked basil stem.

Take remaining fresh basil stem and remove leaves. Stack leaves on top of each other and finely slice and sprinkle over the fish.

Baked Salmon

2 ½ pounds whole salmon, with skin on

1 tablespoon olive oil

Kosher salt and fresh ground pepper

Serves 6-8

Preheat oven to 400 degrees.

Place salmon on parchment lined baking pan with sides. Drizzle the olive oil and rub into salmon. Sprinkle with salt and pepper. Bake for 20 minutes or until the flesh is opaque. Place under the broiler for 5 minutes to crisp the top. Remove from the oven and cut into serving portions.

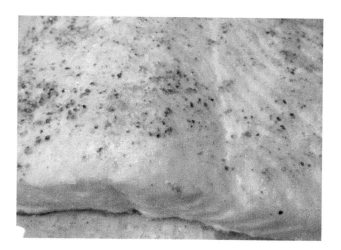

Mushroom Risotto with Shrimp

Risotto:

6 cups low sodium chicken broth

1 ounce dried porcini mushrooms

1 ½ cups hot water

4 ounces cremini mushrooms, coarsely chopped

2 tablespoons butter

1 tablespoon fresh thyme, minced

Kosher salt and black pepper

3 tablespoons olive oil

1 cup onion, minced

2 cups Arborio rice

½ cup dry white wine

2 tablespoons unsalted butter, cut into bits

½ cup fresh grated parmesan cheese

freshly ground black pepper

Heat the broth in a medium sized saucepan and keep it warm over low heat.

Combine the dried mushrooms and hot water in a small bowl. Let stand until mushrooms are softened, about 30 minutes. Once softened, drain the liquid and set mushrooms aside. Coarsely chop the cremini mushrooms.

In a skillet over medium heat, melt the butter. Add the cremini mushrooms. Cook until mushrooms begin to brown. Remove from heat and stir in drained porcini mushrooms and the fresh thyme. Season with salt and pepper.

In a heavy, wide 3 to 4-quart stock pot, heat the olive oil over medium heat. Add the onion and cook until golden, stirring often, about 5 minutes. Add the rice and stir to coat with the oil. Toast the rice until the edges become translucent, 1 to 2 minutes.

Pour in the wine and stir until evaporated. Add ½ cup of the hot stock. Cook, stirring constantly, until all the stock has been absorbed. Continue to add hot stock in small batches, just enough to completely moisten the rice, and cook until each successive batch has been absorbed. Stir constantly and adjust the level of heat so the rice is simmering very gently while adding the stock until the rice mixture is creamy, but al dente. This will take 16-20 minutes from the first addition of stock.

Remove the pan from the heat. Stir in the butter and parmesan cheese until completely melted. Taste for salt and pepper, if needed.

Shrimp:

36 extra-large shrimp, peeled, deveined (about 2 pounds)

Kosher salt and black pepper

2 tablespoons olive oil

1 tablespoon fresh thyme leaves

2 garlic cloves, finely minced

2 tablespoons unsalted butter

Serves 12

Shrimp

Season shrimp with salt and pepper. Drizzle olive oil, thyme and garlic over shrimp. Mix to coat; cover and refrigerate no longer than 1 hour.

Heat butter in a large skillet on high heat. Add about 12 shrimp to the skillet (do not overcrowd) and sauté about 2 minutes on each side. Do not overcook. Shrimp is cooked when it turns pink and the tails slightly curl. Remove first batch and repeat with another batch of shrimp.

Arrange cooked shrimp on top of risotto.

Roasted Potatoes

Vegetables

Vegetable Frittata

1 tablespoon olive oil

1 tablespoon shallot or onion, chopped

1 cup of any pre-cooked vegetable (spinach, asparagus, zucchini, mushrooms, red peppers, potatoes)

6 large eggs

2 tablespoons parmesan cheese

¼ cup provolone/mozzarella cheese, shredded

Pinch of kosher salt, fresh ground pepper

Serves 6

Heat the oil in an 8 inch non-stick pan over medium heat. Add the onion and cook, stirring for 2 -3 minutes. Add the precooked vegetables and distribute evenly in the pan.

In a bowl beat the eggs and cheeses together. Season with salt and pepper. Pour into the pan and cook until the bottom of the frittata is golden and top begins to solidify, 4-5 minutes.

Oven method
Place in a 400 degree oven and bake for 8-10 minutes or until the eggs are set.

Pan fry method
Place a large flat plate over the pan and flip the frittata onto the plate. Slide it back into the pan to cook on the other side. Cook until the bottom is lightly golden, 2-3 minutes. Slide the frittata onto a serving dish.

Serve warm or at room temperature.

Broccoli

1 fresh bunch broccoli

2 tablespoons olive oil

2 cloves garlic, sliced in half

Kosher salt and black pepper

⅓ cup water

Serves 8

Wash and cut the broccoli into florettes with stems about 3-4" long. Heat oil and sliced garlic on high in a frying pan.

Once garlic is golden, flip over the garlic and add the broccoli, salt, pepper and water. Be careful of splattering because oil will be hot.

Cover immediately with a lid and let it cook on high about 5 minutes, until the water completely evaporates.

NOTE: Cauliflower, brocollini or asparagus can be substituted for the broccoli.

Green Beans with Pancetta

3 tablespoons pine nuts

2 pounds fresh green beans, ends trimmed

1 tablespoon olive oil

⅓ pound pancetta or bacon, sliced and cut in ½" strips

⅓ cup chopped shallots or onions

Kosher salt and fresh ground black pepper

Serves 8

In a small dry skillet, cook the pine nuts on medium heat constantly stirring until they start to turn golden. Remove and cool.

Drop fresh green beans into boiling water for 6 minutes.

Meanwhile, add olive oil and pancetta to a large skillet and cook pancetta until almost crispy. Add shallots and sauté until translucent. Remove from heat and hold until beans are ready.

Drain the water and place beans into the pan with the cooked pancetta/shallot mixture. Stir all together. Season with salt and pepper. Cook on med-high heat for about 2 minutes. Top with pine nuts before serving.

Fresh Green Beans

2 pounds fresh green beans, ends trimmed

2 tablespoons olive oil

1 medium onion, chopped

1 clove garlic, finely minced

Kosher salt and black pepper

½ cup water

Serves 8

Prepare beans by trimming off the hard stem ends. Wash in a colander so that beans can drain.

In a large 12" skillet, heat olive oil and cook onion for 3-5 minutes. Add garlic and then the beans. Stir together to completely coat the beans. Season with salt and pepper. Add water and cover with a lid. Cook on high heat for about 6-7 minutes or until all of the water has evaporated.

Transfer to a serving dish.

Sauteed Spinach

3 tablespoons olive oil

1 medium shallot, finely minced

2 cloves garlic, finely minced

1 pound of baby spinach

Kosher salt and pepper

Serves 5-6

In a large skillet, heat olive oil with shallots. Stir shallots for 1 minute and add garlic. Immediately add handfuls of spinach and stir until wilted. Continue to stir and add more spinach until wilted. Repeat until all spinach is wilted. Sprinkle with salt and pepper to taste. Remove from heat and place in a serving dish.

Swiss Chard, Potatoes & Beans

3 bunches of swiss chard

¼ cup olive oil

3 medium potatoes (peeled and cubed)

2 cloves garlic, finely minced

1 can (15.5 ounce) cannellini beans, drained and rinsed

1 can (14.5 ounce) chicken or vegetable broth

Kosher salt and black pepper

Serves 8

Remove thick stems from swiss chard by holding the top of the stem and pulling your other hand down the stem to remove the leaf. Tear leaves into 4" pieces. Wash swiss chard in cold water and shake off excess water. Set aside in a colandar.

In a 6 quart dutch oven pot, heat olive oil. On high heat cook and stir potatoes until golden on both sides. Remove potatoes to another dish. Season with salt and pepper. Add garlic and stir; immediately add two handfuls of swiss chard. Be careful of splattering. Stir and let it wilt before adding 2 more handfuls. Continue to add until all swiss chard is in the pan. Add potatoes, beans and chicken broth. Bring to a boil and reduce heat to a simmer. Cover with a lid and cook for 8 minutes until swiss chard is tender. Add salt and pepper to taste.

Serve with corn bread.

Green Peas with Shallots & Pancetta

2 tablespoons olive oil

⅓ pound pancetta, cut into small dice

2 shallots, halved and thinly sliced

1 small clove garlic, finely minced

1 pound frozen peas, thawed

Serves 4-6

Heat the oil in a saute pan over medium heat. Add the pancetta and cook until golden brown and the fat has rendered. Remove the pancetta to a plate lined with paper towels.

Add the shallots to the pan and cook until soft. Add the garlic, then the peas and cook until warmed through. Return the browned pancetta to the peas in the pan. Transfer to a serving bowl.

Fresh Corn with Red Pepper

3 tablespoons butter

1 medium shallot, finely minced

½ red pepper, diced

4 fresh corn on the cob, kernels cut off or 1lb bag of frozen corn

1 tablespoon fresh basil leaves, sliced into thin ribbons

Kosher salt and pepper

Serves 6

In a 12 inch fry pan heat butter until melted and add shallot and red pepper. Cook for a few minutes until softened.

Add corn and stir until corn is mixed in and starts to caramelize, about 4-5 minutes. Sprinkle salt and pepper to taste. Add fresh basil just before serving.

Cheesy Potatoes

Onions:

1 tablespoon butter

½ small onion, chopped

Potatoes:

2 pounds frozen shredded potatoes or hash brown potatoes

16 ounces sour cream

6 tablespoons butter, melted

1 can (10 ounce) cream of chicken soup

8 ounces sharp cheddar cheese, grated

Salt and pepper to taste

9x13 pan sprayed with vegetable spray

Serves 12

Onions
Cook the onion in the butter until the onions are translucent, about 4-5 minutes.

Potatoes
Mix all of the ingredients in a large bowl and pour into the prepared pan.

Bake at 375 for 45-60 minutes or until all of the edges are slightly golden brown and it is bubbling in the middle.

This can be made the night before and stored in the refrigerator. Bake the next day.

Roasted Potatoes

1 ½ pounds small potatoes (Red skin or Yukon Gold), washed

3 tablespoons olive oil

2 tablespoons fresh rosemary, finely minced

1 clove garlic, finely minced

2 pinches of Kosher salt and freshly ground black pepper

Serves 6

Preheat oven to 400 degrees. Wash and cut potatoes in half. (If using larger potatoes, cut into smaller pieces.) Place in a bowl and add olive oil, rosemary, garlic, salt and pepper. Toss to evenly coat and pour into a jelly roll pan with sides.

Reposition potatoes so that cut sides are down on the pan. Bake at 400 degrees for 45 minutes. Potatoes should have a golden brown color. Remove with a spatula and place in a serving dish.

Roasted Root Vegetables with Gremolata

Gremolata:

½ cup finely chopped parsley

Zest of a lemon

1 teaspoon garlic, finely minced

Root Vegetables:

4 carrots, peeled and cut in half

4 parsnips, peeled and cut in half

1 sweet potato, peeled and cubed

8 red potatoes, cut in half

3 medium shallots, cut in half

1 tablespoon fresh thyme leaves

¼ cup olive oil

Kosher salt and freshly ground pepper

Serves 8

Preheat oven to 400 degrees.

Gremolata
Toss the parsley, lemon zest, and garlic in a bowl, cover and set aside.

Root Vegetables
Place the vegetables in a large bowl and toss with thyme, olive oil, salt, and several grinds of pepper. Arrange the vegetables in a single layer on a rimmed baking sheet and roast until they are tender and ever so slightly browned, 35-45 minutes. Remove from the oven and toss in the gremolata.

Potatoes with Parmesan Cheese & Eggs

3 large eggs

½ cup parmesan cheese, grated

3 medium russet potatoes, peel and sliced into ¼" rounds

2 tablespoons corn oil

Kosher salt and fresh ground black pepper

Serves 6

Beat the eggs and parmesan cheese together. Set aside.

Heat oil in a 12" skillet. Add half of the potatoes so that all of the slices are touching the bottom of the pan. Cook until brown on one side then flip over and brown the other side. Remove to a dish and season with salt and pepper. Cook the remaining potatoes in the same manner. Keep the browned potatoes in the pan. Season with salt and pepper. Add the cooked potatoes in the dish to the skillet.

Pour the parmesan cheese/egg mixture over the top of the potatoes. Let sit for 2 minutes before you stir the egg mixture in. Flip over pieces of potatoes that are coated with the egg mixture. Continue to cook over medium heat until the eggs are cooked.

Yukon Gold Mashed Potatoes

3 pounds Yukon gold potatoes

1 tablespoon Kosher salt

4 tablespoons butter

4 tablespoons olive oil

½ cup half and half

1 tablespoon fresh parsley, finely minced

1 tablespoon fresh chives, finely minced

Kosher salt and black pepper to taste

Serves 8

Wash and cut potatoes with skins into 6-8 pieces. Place cut potatoes in a stock pan with cold water; add the Kosher salt. Bring to a boil and cook for about 20-30 minutes or until potatoes are fork tender.

Drain the water and mash with a potato masher or stir in a mixer on low speed using a paddle. Add the butter and olive oil to the potatoes. Taste for additional salt and pepper.

Once the butter is melted and mixed in, add the half and half, parsely and chives. Stir until potatoes are smooth.

Twice Baked Potatoes

8 medium Russet potatoes

8 tablespoons butter

1 cup sour cream

⅓ cup whole milk

1 cup sharp cheddar cheese, grated

Kosher salt and black pepper to taste

Serves 8

Preheat oven to 400 degrees. Pierce potatoes with a knife. Place potatoes on a baking sheet and bake for 1 hour. Remove from oven and reduce heat to 375 degrees.

Place the butter, sour cream, milk and cheese in a medium size bowl.

Cut potatoes in half lengthwise while they are still hot and scoop out the flesh of the potato with a spoon and add to the bowl. Be careful to leave some of the potato in the skin so the shell stays together.

Mash the potatoes with a fork and continue until all potatoes have been mashed. Season with salt and pepper. Stir the mixture until all ingredients are mixed in.

Refill the shells with the potato mixture and place the filled potatoes back on the baking sheet. Bake for 15-20 minutes.

My Fresh Berry pie

Desserts

Almond Butter Crescents

2 ¼ cups all-purpose flour

¼ teaspoon salt

¾ cup finely chopped almonds, toasted (about ½ cup whole almonds)

1 cup butter

½ cup sugar

1 large egg yolk

2 teaspoons vanilla extract

8 ounces semi-sweet chocolate

Yields 50-55 cookies

Preheat oven to 375 degrees.

In a bowl, stir together flour, salt, and almonds.

In a mixer, cream butter and sugar until light and fluffy. Blend in egg yolk and vanilla extract. Gradually add flour mixture on low speed just until dough clings together. Remove dough from mixer and place in a bowl to finish mixing by hand the flour into the dough.

Pinch off a small piece of dough for each cookie and roll into a 1" ball. Roll dough between the palms of your hands into a snake with tapered ends. Place on a parchment lined baking sheet and bend into a crescent moon shape. Bake for 12-15 minutes or until the ends are golden. Remove and allow to cool.

Heat chocolate in microwave or on top of double-boiler until smooth. Dip the top third of the cookie at an angle into the chocolate. Allow the excess to drip off and gently scrape the bottom against the side to remove extra chocolate. Place on parchment paper and let chocolate set to dry. You can refrigerate the tray to speed up this process.

Amaretti

1 pound blanched almonds, whole

1 ⅓ cups sugar

3 large egg whites

1 tablespoon almond extract

Extra sugar for rolling (about ½ cup)

Yields 30 cookies

Preheat oven to 325 degrees.

Place almonds and sugar in a food processor and grind until very fine. You are looking for almond flour. Transfer to a medium bowl and stir in the egg whites and almond extract with a spatula until all is incorporated. The dough should be slightly sticky but should be stiff enough for rolling into balls. If it is too dry, add a little more egg white. Mix in and see if the dough is slightly sticky but solid enough to roll into balls. If the dough is too sticky, you will have to add more ground almonds so that the dough is stiff enough to roll.

Dampen the palms of your hands with a little water and press them into sugar. This helps to prevent the mixture from sticking to your hands.

Roll into 1 ½ inch balls (almost the size of a ping pong ball) and then roll to completely coat in the dish of extra sugar.

Place on the baking sheet lined with parchment paper and bake for 22-25 minutes or until they are slightly golden on top.

A perfect Amaretti should slightly rise, be a nice dome shape and full of cracks on the surface.

Apricot Filled Squares

Dough:

3 cups all-purpose flour

⅛ teaspoon salt

¼ cup sugar

½ teaspoon baking powder

1 cup butter (2 sticks), cold and cut into ½"cubes

3 large egg yolks

2 tablespoons sour cream

1 teaspoon orange zest

1 teaspoon vanilla

Apricot Filling:

2 cups dried apricots

1 ¾ - 2 cups orange juice

¾ cup sugar

Yields 30 cookies

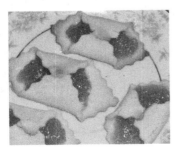

Dough

In a food processor, mix flour, salt, sugar and baking powder. Add butter and pulse for 10 (1 second) pulses to mix until mealy as for a pie crust. Add egg yolks, sour cream, orange zest and vanilla. Use short pulses until dough starts to form into a ball. Remove dough from bowl and divide into 3 balls. Flatten into a 5" disk and wrap each disk with plastic wrap. Chill for at least 1 hour or overnight is best.

Roll out one disk of dough on a lightly floured board and cut into 2-inch squares with a pizza cutter. Place about a teaspoon of the apricot filling in the middle of the square. Fold up and pinch together opposite corners of square and place on cookie sheet. Bake at 350 for 10 minutes until edges are lightly golden. Dust with powdered sugar before serving.

Apricot Filling
This can be made ahead and refrigerated.

Cut dried apricots in 4 pieces with kitchen shears. Put into a sauce pan with lid. Add the orange juice and bring to a boil. Cover and lower heat to a very slow simmer. Simmer 50 minutes stirring occasionally. Once most of the orange juice has evaporated, add the sugar and continue cooking for 5 more minutes. Continue stirring so it does not stick or burn. This also helps to break down the apricots. Apricot mixture should be thick. Remove from heat and set aside to cool.

Blondies

1 cup whole pecans

12 tablespoons (1 ½ sticks) unsalted butter

1 ½ cups all-purpose flour

1 teaspoon baking powder

½ teaspoon salt

1 ½ cups packed light brown sugar

2 large eggs

4 teaspoons vanilla extract

½ cup white chocolate chips

⅔ cup semi-sweet chocolate chips

Yields 30 triangles

Preheat oven to 350 degrees. Spread nuts on large rimmed baking sheet and bake until nuts are toasted about 10-14 minutes. Transfer nuts to cutting board to cool; chop coarsely and set aside.

Heat butter in 10" skillet over medium-high heat until melted, about 2 minutes. Continue cooking, swirling pan frequently until butter is dark golden brown and has nutty aroma, 4 to 6 minutes. Remove skillet from heat and transfer browned butter to another bowl and allow to cool.

While nuts toast, place a piece of parchment paper to fit into a 9"x13" baking pan.

Whisk flour, baking powder and salt together in medium bowl, set aside.

Whisk melted butter and brown sugar together in a medium bowl until combined. Add eggs and vanilla and mix well. Using rubber spatula, fold dry ingredients into egg mixture until just combined; do not over mix. Fold in white chocolate, semi-sweet chocolate and nuts. Pour batter into prepared pan, smoothing top with rubber spatula until evenly distributed.

Bake until top is shiny and cracked, and light golden brown, 22-25 minutes; do not over bake. Cool on wire rack to room temperature. Remove bars from pan by lifting the parchment paper. Cut into 3" squares (about 15) and then into triangles and serve.

Clothespin Cookies

Cookie Dough:

2 cups all-purpose flour

½ teaspoon table salt

1 tablespoons sugar

1 cup unsalted butter, cold and cut into ½" cubes

1 large egg yolk

1 cup sour cream

Filling:

7 ounces marshmallow crème

8 ounces cream cheese, room temperature

4 tablespoons butter, softened

⅔ cup powdered sugar

1 teaspoon vanilla extract

Yields 48 cookies

Cookie Dough

In a food processor, pulse flour, salt, sugar and butter for 10 one-second pulses. Butter should be no bigger than the size of green peas. Mix egg yolks with sour cream and pulse into the butter/flour mixture until a ball of dough starts to form. Separate the dough into 4 equal parts and press each into a 4" square. Cover with plastic wrap and refrigerate overnight.

Preheat oven to 400 degrees. Cover wooden clothespins (no springs) with heavy duty foil and spray lightly with vegetable spray. Place parchment paper onto jelly roll pans with sides.

Roll out one piece of dough between 2 lightly floured pieces of parchment paper. Roll into a rectangle 7"x11". Cut into 12 strips ¾" wide. Place one strip on the open end of the clothespin diagonally. Wrap the clothespin at an angle slightly overlapping the dough until you use up the strip. Press gently at the end to secure. Place clothespins 2 inches apart onto the prepared pan. Refrigerate the ones that are complete until you have a pan ready for the oven. Repeat with the other pieces in the refrigerator.

Bake for 13-15 minutes or until golden brown. Remove the cookie from the clothespin while still warm. Cool before filling.

Filling

Mix all together in a standing mixer with a paddle on medium speed.

Fill the cooled cookies using a pastry bag or a plastic freezer bag with one corner cut off. Dust with powdered sugar.

Fruit & Nut Crescent Cookies

Cookie Dough:

2 ½ cups all-purpose flour

½ teaspoon salt

16 tablespoons (2 sticks) cold unsalted butter, ½" cubes

1 cup sour cream

2 large egg yolks

1 teaspoon yeast

Filling:

1 cup apricot jam

½ cup peach jam

½ cup pineapple preserves

Zest of one orange

2 cups walnut halves, toasted and then finely ground

Topping:

2 large egg whites

Yields 48 cookies

Cookie Dough

In a food processor, add flour, salt, and cubed butter. Process for seven (1 second) short pulses. Add sour cream, egg yolks, and yeast and process for seven additional (1 second) pulses. Keep using short pulses until flour is incorporated and dough starts to hold together.

Remove dough from work bowl and put into another large bowl. Start pressing the dough together to pick up any crumbs. Divide the dough in half. Then divide each piece into 3 equal pieces (total of 6). Flatten each piece into a 6" disk onto plastic wrap. Wrap and stack into a plastic disposable bag. Place in refrigerator overnight.

Filling

Preheat oven to 350 degrees. Place walnuts in a single layer on a cookie sheet and bake in the oven for 12-15 minutes, or until toasted. Remove and cool before finely grinding in a food processor. Mix all of the filling ingredients together and set aside.

Rolling

Roll out a disk of dough on parchment paper and sprinkle with powdered sugar. Roll each disk into an 8" circle. Spread about ¼ cup of filling around the outside of the circle. The center circle should be without filling. Cut into 8 pieces. Roll each triangle into a crescent. Press the point into the crescent. Place on parchment lined cookie sheets with points down and outer edges curved. Brush lightly with egg white before baking.

Bake at 400 degrees for about 11-14 minutes or until light golden brown. As soon as they are removed from the oven, carefully move them with an off-set spatula so they do not stick to the parchment paper because filling has come out. Allow to cool before storing in an air-tight container.

Fig Filled Cookies

Filling:

1 cup (6 ounces) dried mission figs (black), ends trimmed and cut in half

1 cup (6 ounces) dried calimyrna figs (green), ends trimmed and cut in half

1 cup (5 ounces) chopped dates

1 cup apricot jam

Zest of 1 orange

Juice of 1 orange juice

1 teaspoon cinnamon

1 cup whole walnuts, toasted

½ cup raisins

Dough:

4 cups all-purpose flour

½ cup sugar

1 teaspoon baking powder

½ teaspoon salt

8 tablespoon butter, cold & cubed

8 tablespoon Crisco, cold & cubed

1 large egg

½ cup whole milk

1 teaspoon vanilla extract

Filling

In a food processor, combine all the filling ingredients until coarsely pureed, about one minute; if the mixture begins to clump, stop and redistribute the contents as necessary. If the mixture seems dry, add about one tablespoon more orange juice. (The filling may be refrigerated for up to 4 days; let come to room temperature and stir before using.)

Dough

In a food processor, combine the flour, sugar, baking powder and salt. Drop butter and Crisco over flour and pulse 10-15 one second pulses or until the mixture is the consistency of coarse meal. Pour milk, egg and vanilla into bowl and process in on/off pulses just until evenly incorporated; do not over process. Working on a sheet of wax paper, knead until a smooth, slightly moist but not wet dough forms. If the dough is too dry or crumbly to hold together easily, sprinkle on a little water, 1-2 teaspoons at a time, and continue kneading. If the dough is too sticky, add a little more flour.

Divide the dough in half. Flatten into 6" squares. Wrap in plastic and refrigerate 20-30 minutes. Take out one disk and cut in half. On lightly floured parchment paper, roll the cut piece into a 9" square. Cut and patch the dough as necessary to even the sides. Cut into three 3"x9" strips. Spoon about ¼ cup of the filling down the length of each strip, keeping the filling in the middle. Fold the sides of each strip over the filling and the folded over portions meet, then lightly press down on the seam to seal. Cut each log into 6 pieces. Place on cookie sheet. Cut three slits on top of cookie. Brush with egg white. Repeat with remaining pieces of dough.

1 large egg white for brushing the tops of each cookie

Icing:

¾ cup powdered sugar

1-2 tablespoons half and half

½ teaspoon vanilla extract

1 tablespoon butter, softened

1 jar of colored sprinkles

Yields 75 (1 ½" cookies)

Bake in 375 degree oven for 15-19 minutes or until browned on the bottoms and slightly darker at the edges. Remove and cool.

Icing

Mix icing ingredients together until smooth and place in a freezer quart size bag. Zip shut and squeeze out air. Twist the bag down to the icing. Cut a small corner off of one side and squeeze to drizzle diagonal lines over each cookie.

Florentine Cookies

½ cup whipping cream

2 tablespoons honey

½ cup sugar

4 tablespoons butter

1 ½ cups sliced almonds, rough chopped

Zest of one orange

½ cup all-purpose flour

12 ounces semi-sweet chocolate

Yields 48 cookies

Position the rack in the center of the oven and preheat the oven to 350 degrees.

Line a baking sheet with parchment paper. Stir the cream, honey, sugar and butter in a heavy medium saucepan over medium heat until the sugar dissolves. Bring the mixture to a boil. Boil for one minute. Remove the pan from the heat and stir in the almonds, zest and flour.

Drop ½ of a teaspoon into mounds about 3 inches apart onto the parchment paper (the cookies will spread). Flatten the batter slightly with a wet spatula.

Bake the cookies until they are lacy and golden brown, about 9 minutes. Remove them from the oven and let them stand for about 5 minutes. Remove the cookies to a wire rack, let them cool completely, and spread them with melted chocolate. (The cookies can be made up to this point 2 months ahead. Cool completely, then store airtight in the freezer. Defrost before continuing.)

Stir the chocolate in a bowl set over a saucepan of simmering water until the chocolate melts. Spread a thin layer of melted chocolate on the flat side of each cookie. Make decorative swirls with a fork or decorating comb. Set cookies on parchment paper until chocolate sets. Repeat with the remaining cookies and chocolate.

Italian Pistachio Cookies

¾ cup pistachios, toasted

⅔ cup sugar

1 cup blanched almond meal or almond flour

2 large egg whites

Topping:

1 cup pistachios (raw, shelled and roughly chopped)

Yields 24 cookies

Preheat oven to 325 degrees on convection heat. Place ¾ cup of pistachios in a single layer on a baking sheet. Bake for about 8-10 minutes until toasted. Cool completely and reserve.

Place the toasted pistachios and sugar in the food processor and finely chop. Add the blanched almond meal and egg whites. The dough should form a paste. (If the batter is too sticky, add a little bit more of the almond meal or if it is too dry add a little more egg white.)

Scoop the cookie batter and form into 1" balls. Roll the balls in the roughly chopped raw pistachios and coat completely.

Place the cookies 2" apart on a parchment lined baking sheet.

Bake in a convection oven (325 degrees) for about 16-20 minutes. Cookies should be golden around the edges and on top.

Orange Almond Biscotti

½ cup butter

1 cup sugar

3 large eggs

2 teaspoons vanilla extract

Finely grated zest of an orange

2½ cups all-purpose flour

2 teaspoons baking powder

1 cup whole almonds, toasted (approximately 4 ounces)

6 ounces semi-sweet chocolate

Yields 25 biscotti

Line a baking sheet with parchment paper. Preheat oven to 350° degrees.

Cream together the butter and sugar until fluffy. Beat in the eggs and vanilla and orange zest. Add the flour and baking powder and mix just until incorporated. Fold in the nuts with a spatula.

Divide the dough in half and shape into two logs about 4 inches wide and ¾ inches high. Place them 2 inches apart. Bake in a 350°F oven for 30 minutes or until they are lightly puffed and browned. Cool for 10 minutes on the pan. Carefully peel off parchment paper and transfer to a cutting board. With a serrated knife, cut each log diagonally into ¾ -inch slices. Place them back on the cookie sheet and bake for an additional 15 minutes. Cool.

Dip one end diagonally into melted chocolate, brush melted chocolate on one side or drizzle chocolate diagonally on the side. Refrigerate for 10-15 minutes to allow chocolate to harden.

Can be stored in an air-tight container for a few weeks.

Pecan Tarts

Tart dough:

8 ounces cream cheese, softened

3 sticks unsalted butter, softened

3 cups all-purpose flour

Filling:

2 cups pecans, toasted and roughly chopped

3 cups whole pecans, toasted

4 large eggs, lightly beaten

1 cup brown sugar

1 cup light corn syrup

4 tablespoons butter, melted

1 tablespoon vanilla extract

A pinch of salt

Yields 72 pecan tarts

Dough

Cream butter and cream cheese together in a mixer. Stir in flour until all is incorporated. Shape into 1" balls. Refrigerate for at least 1 hour.

Prepare 6 mini-muffin tins by lightly coating with cooking spray. Place one ball into each muffin cup and press against the bottom and up the sides to form a tart shell.

Filling

Sprinkle chopped pecans into individual mini cups. Stir all of the filling ingredients together. Place filling into a pouring measuring cup. Then pour filling into the individual cups until ⅔ full. Top with a whole pecan.

Bake at 375 degrees for 15 minutes or until crust is golden brown. Let cool in pan before removing.

Note: These tarts can be frozen in an airtight container for one month.

Pine Nut Cookies

15 ounces almond paste

1 teaspoon vanilla extract

1 cup superfine sugar

2 large egg whites, room temp.

Pinch salt

1 cup (5 ounces) pine nuts

Yields 25 cookies

Preheat oven to 325 degrees. Line 2 cookie trays with parchment paper.

Break the almond paste into chunks and place in the bowl of a food processor. Add the vanilla and sugar and process until the mixture is homogenous, stopping once to scrape down the bowl using a rubber spatula. Add the egg whites and salt; process until smooth. Scrape again and process for a few more seconds or just until incorporated.

The mixture will be sticky, but with a light touch and moist hands it can be gently rolled. Keep a damp towel nearby to wipe and wet your hands. Using damp hands, round the mix into scant 1-inch balls and drop the balls into a shallow bowl of pine nuts. Quickly lift and flip batter "no nuts" side down onto cookie sheet.

Bake the first tray while preparing the second, until the cookies are lightly golden, about 15-17 minutes. Place the baking sheets on wire cooling racks and cool the cookies completely before lifting them off. Store in an airtight container for up to 2 days, or freeze for up to 1 month.

Pineapple Cookies

8 ounces cream cheese, room temperature

3 sticks butter, softened

¼ cup sugar

3 cups all-purpose flour

2 jars (12 ounces) pineapple preserves

Yields 50-55 cookies

With a mixer, cream butter, sugar and cream cheese together. Add flour gradually on lowest speed and mix just until incorporated.

Separate dough into three balls and flatten into 6 inch disks. Cover each disk with plastic wrap and refrigerate for at least one hour.

Remove one of the pieces of dough from the refrigerator and place it on parchment paper that is lightly floured. Place a pinch of flour on top of the disk and another piece of parchment paper. Roll it out into a 10 inch circle. If dough sticks, sprinkle a pinch of flour or place on cookie sheet in the freezer to chill. Cut out 2 inch circles and reserve scraps to re-roll. Place in plastic wrap and back in the refrigerator. Place 1 teaspoon of pineapple preserves in the middle of the circle. Fold over and press edges with a fork to seal.

Place on a cookie sheet lined with parchment paper.

Bake at 375 degrees for 12-15 minutes or until golden on top.

Remove from oven and move each cookie slightly away from the filling that may have leaked out. Let them cool completely before sprinkling with powdered sugar.

Pizzelle Cookies

6 large eggs

1 ¾ cups sugar

3 tablespoons vanilla or anise extract

1 cup butter, melted

4 teaspoons baking powder

3 ½ cups all-purpose flour

Yields 50-55 cookies

Beat eggs, sugar and extract together until light and fluffy. Add melted butter on low speed. Then add baking powder and flour and mix just until incorporated. Let dough sit at room temperature about 15 minutes.

Drop a full teaspoon of dough into the middle of a pre-heated and greased pizzelle iron. Bake just until golden. Remove to a cooling rack and repeat until all of the cookies are baked.

Store the cookies in an air-tight container for up to 1 month.

Ricotta Iced Cookies

Cookie dough:

1 ½ cups sugar

1 cup butter, softened

15 ounces ricotta cheese

1 tablespoon vanilla extract

2 large eggs

3 ¾ cups all-purpose flour

1 tablespoon baking powder

pinch of salt

Icing:

1 ½ cups powdered sugar

3 tablespoons half and half

1 teaspoon vanilla extract

Assorted colored sprinkles

Yields 48 cookies

Dough

Preheat oven to 350 degrees. Cream butter and sugar until light and fluffy. Add ricotta, vanilla, and eggs until well combined.

On low speed, add flour, baking powder, and salt. Mix just until incorporated. Do not over mix.

Drop dough by teaspoons about 2" apart onto cookie sheet. Bake about 12 to 15 minutes or until cookies are lightly golden on the bottom and around the edges (cookies will be soft).

When cookies are cool, prepare icing and spread on cookies. Sprinkle with colored sugar or jimmies before icing sets. Let dry before placing into an airtight container.

Icing

Stir ingredients together until smooth. A little more half and half may be added until you have the correct spreading consistency.

Decorate with colored sprinkles.

Sour Cream Cookies

Dough

1 ½ cups sugar

1 cup butter (2 sticks), room temperature

2 large eggs

1 tablespoon vanilla extract

1 cup sour cream

3 teaspoons baking powder

1 teaspoon baking soda

4 cups all-purpose flour

Assembly

½ cup granulated sugar to roll cookies in

1 cup powdered sugar to roll cookies in

Topping

1 jar maraschino cherries (10 ounces), drain and cut in half; dry between paper towels.

Yields 60-75 cookies

Dough

Cream butter and sugar until light and fluffy. Add eggs one at a time and mix until incorporated. Add vanilla and sour cream and continue to mix until smooth. On low speed, mix all dry ingredients just until incorporated.

Place cookie dough in refrigerator for at least 2 hours or overnight.

Assembly

Remove chilled dough from refrigerator and roll into 1" balls. Roll in granulated sugar and then heavily roll in powdered sugar until coated completely. Place on cookie sheet a few inches apart. Lightly press cherry half into the center of each ball. Bake for 10-12 minutes at 350 degrees. Bottoms and edges should be a light golden color.

Note: This cookie can be made without the cherries.

Taralucci (Anise Cookies)

Dough

6 large eggs

1 ¼ cups sugar

½ cup canola or vegetable oil

2 tablespoons whole anise seeds

5 cups all-purpose flour, plus
   more if needed

Assembly

1 large egg white, beaten lightly

Yields 80 cookies

Dough

Beat eggs on high speed for 5 minutes. Add sugar and oil and continue to beat until light and fluffy. Add the fennel and flour; mix on low to form a ball of dough. More flour may be needed to make a smooth dough that is not too sticky.

Assembly

Pinch off a piece of dough about the size of a quarter. Roll into a snake about 4" long and press the ends together to form a circle.

Drop into boiling water. Use a spatula once it touches the bottom and loosen it. When it floats to the top, take it out with a slotted spoon. Place on a towel to absorb excess water.

Transfer cookies to parchment lined cookie sheets and brush lightly with the egg white. Bake at 375 degrees for 25 minutes or until golden brown. Turn up the heat to 400 degrees and bake for an additional 10 minutes until the cookies are golden brown.

Triple Chocolate Almond Biscotti

8 tablespoons unsalted butter, softened

1 ¼ cups sugar

2 teaspoons vanilla extract

3 large eggs

Pinch of salt

½ cup unsweetened cocoa

2 cups all-purpose flour

2 teaspoons baking powder

6 ounces semi-sweet chocolate chips

1 cup whole almonds, toasted

6 ounces white chocolate

Yields 25 biscotti

Preheat the oven to 350 degrees and set the rack in the middle of the oven. Cover a large cookie sheet with parchment paper.

Beat the butter, sugar, and vanilla with an electric mixer on medium to high speed for a few minutes. Add the eggs, one at a time and then the salt. Stop mixer and scrape the sides down and beat for 1 minute. On lowest speed, add the cocoa, flour, baking powder and mix just until incorporated. Stir in the chocolate chips and almonds.

Spoon the dough onto the prepared pan in two strips, each about 2 inches wide and the length of the pan.

Bake the logs of dough about 30-35 minutes, or until they are well risen and have also spread to about double in size. The logs are done when pressed with a fingertip they feel firm. Cool on cookie sheet for 1 hour.

Transfer the logs to a cutting board. Using a serrated knife, cut each of the rolls diagonally into ½ "thick slices. Place the slices, cut sides down, on the cookie sheet. Bake the biscotti for 15-20 minutes at 350 degrees or until they are dry and crisp. Transfer to a wire rack and cool.

Melt the white chocolate. Dip each end on the diagonal into the melted chocolate and scrape off excess on the bottom. Place on a parchment lined cookie sheet and allow the chocolate to harden. Store the biscotti between sheets of parchment paper in a tin or plastic container with a tight fitting lid.

White Chocolate Raspberry Cookies

Dough

4 ounce white chocolate, melted

1 cup butter (2 sticks), softened

⅔ cup sugar

2 teaspoons vanilla extract

1 large egg yolk, room temp.

1 teaspoon baking powder

2 ¼ cups all-purpose flour

Topping

10 ounces seedless red

 raspberry jam

4 ounces white chocolate

Yields 60-75 cookies

Preheat oven to 375 degrees.

Dough

In a double boiler, melt the white chocolate over low heat until smooth. Cool slightly.

In a mixer, cream butter, sugar and vanilla until light and fluffy. With mixer running on low speed, add melted chocolate and continue until all of the chocolate is mixed in well. Add the egg yolk and mix in. With mixer on lowest speed, add baking powder and flour just until incorporated.

Drop ½ teaspoon of dough 2 inches apart onto parchment lined cookie sheets. Bake cookies for 7-9 minutes. They should be lightly golden around the edges. Remove from oven; immediately press lightly in the center with a wooden tart press while cookies are still hot.

Topping

In a small saucepan heat and stir the jam over low heat until melted and smooth. Spoon about ½ teaspoon of jam on top of each cookie to fill in the indentation.

In a double boiler, melt the white chocolate over low heat until smooth. Place melted chocolate in a pint size plastic freezer bag. Zip shut and squeeze out the air. Twist the bag down to the chocolate. Cut a very small corner off of one side and squeeze to drizzle diagonal lines over each cookie.

Let chocolate set before moving to a container. Store cookies in an air-tight container with sheets of parchment paper between layers of cookies.

Strawberry & Ladyfinger Dessert

One 9" springform pan

2 (3 ounce) packages soft ladyfingers

⅓ cup orange liqueur

2 cups heavy whipping cream

2 tablespoons powdered sugar

2 packets Whip It (.35 ounce)

1 teaspoon vanilla extract

1 teaspoon orange zest, grated

⅓ cup seedless strawberry jam,
plus 1 tablespoon more for
brushing on top of strawberry

1 pound strawberries, thinly
sliced (reserve 1 whole berry
for the center)

Serves 10

Line the bottom of the pan with 18 ladyfingers. Cut a few to completely cover the bottom. Lightly brush the ladyfingers with the orange liqueur. Line the sides of the mold with more ladyfingers, standing them up, with the lightly browned side facing outward. Lightly brush the ladyfingers with the orange liqueur.

In a mixer fitted with a whisk, beat the heavy cream, powdered sugar, Whip It, and vanilla until stiff peaks form. Add the orange zest and strawberry jam and continue to whisk in until smooth.

Carefully fill the pan with the cream. Use an off-set spatula to smooth out the top and spread the filling evenly. Place a layer of sliced strawberries overlapping each other in circles on top. Place the reserved whole strawberry in the center. Brush strawberry jam on top of the berries.

Cover with plastic wrap and refrigerate for at least one hour.

To serve: Remove the sides of the pan and transfer the dessert to a platter. Slice and serve.

Vanilla Gelato (Ice Cream)

2 ½ cups whole milk

1 cup heavy whipping cream

½ cup sugar

2 tablespoons corn syrup

pinch of salt

1 vanilla bean

4 egg yolks

¼ cup sugar

Yields 1 ½ quarts

In a medium saucepan, combine the milk, heavy cream, ½ cup sugar, corn syrup and pinch of salt. Split the vanilla bean lengthwise to open, scrape out seeds and add the seeds with the pod to the pan with the cream. Stir to break up. Heat over medium heat and bring the mixture to a simmer, stirring occasionally.

In a mixing bowl, whisk the egg yolks and the ¼ cup sugar until they lighten in color. Temper the egg mixture by gradually adding small amounts of the hot milk mixture to the egg mixture. Return the entire mixture to the saucepan and place over medium heat. Continue to cook, stirring frequently, until the mixture thickens slightly, about 5 minutes.

Pour the mixture into a container passing through a sieve to catch the pod and any imperfections. Place in the refrigerator 4-8 hours or overnight.

Pour into an ice cream maker and process according to manufacturer's directions. This process should take about 25-35 minutes. Serve immediately and freeeze the ice cream in air-tight container.

Torrone Almond Nougat

1½ cups whole almonds, toasted

1½ cups hazelnuts, toasted and skins removed

2 sheets rice paper (8½-x11-inches)

1 cup light corn syrup

¾ cup sugar

⅓ cup water

⅓ cup honey

2 large egg whites, room temp.

⅓ cup powdered sugar

1 tablespoon vanilla extract

Yields 60-75 pieces

Preparing the nuts

Preheat oven to 350°F and place the almonds on a cookie sheet. Bake 12-14 minutes or until toasted. On another cookie sheet, bake the hazelnuts 12 minutes or until toasted and fragrant. Remove hazelnuts from oven and place on a clean, dry towel. Cover and rub the nuts with the towel to remove the skins. Set both aside.

Assembly

Line a glass 9"x13"x2" pan with plastic wrap so it overlaps on all sides. Place one sheet of rice paper in the bottom of the pan (shiny side up).

Combine corn syrup, sugar, and water in a saucepan. Clip a candy thermometer to the side of the pan making sure it does not touch the bottom. Cook over medium heat until the temperature reaches 280°degrees (15 minutes). Pour the honey into the syrup and stir. Cook, stirring occasionally, until it reaches the hard crack stage and a candy thermometer registers 315 degrees. Remove from the heat and stir until the temperature drops to 300 degrees, 1 to 2 minutes.

Meanwhile, in the bowl of an electric mixer, beat the egg whites until soft peaks form. Add powdered sugar and vanilla and beat until stiff peaks form. With the mixer running, slowly pour the hot mixture into the meringue down the side of the work bowl so it does not splash out. This will cause the meringue to double in volume. Continue beating the mixture for at least 5-6 minutes until thick and mixture has cooled. Fold in the almonds and hazelnuts.

Working quickly, pour into the pan and spread out evenly over rice paper. Use plastic gloves that have been sprayed with non-stick vegetable spray to help make this easier. The filling is sticky. Cover with another piece of rice paper (shiny side down) and press to evenly distribute the filling. Cover with the plastic wrap in pan and place weights on nougat. Set it aside for a few hours.

Uncover and turn the nougat out of the pan onto a cutting board. Cut the nougat into squares or diamond shapes. Store in an airtight container in layers, separated by wax paper or parchment paper. Keep the nougat at room temperature for up to 2 weeks.

NOTE: All almonds can be used instead of almonds/hazelnuts. Increase to 3 cups.

Cannoli

1 pound whole milk ricotta (page 175) drained overnight

⅔ cup heavy whipping cream

⅔ cup powdered sugar, plus extra for dusting

1 teaspoon vanilla extract

¼ cup mini chocolate chips plus ½ cup for dipping ends in

2 packages of cannoli shells (12 large or 24 mini shells)

Yields 12 large or 24 small

In a food processor, process ricotta until smooth. Remove from the food processor to another bowl.

In a mixing bowl fitted with a whisk, whip the heavy cream, powdered sugar and vanilla until stiff peaks form.

Fold the whipped cream and mini chocolate chips into the ricotta.

Working from either end, fill the cannoli shell with the ricotta filling using a pastry bag or a plastic bag with a hole cut in the end. Press gently to ensure the middle is filled. Dip both ends of cannoli into chocolate chips. Sprinkle generously with powdered sugar. Refrigerate before serving.

Note: If using store bought ricotta, purchase "whole milk" ricotta. You will need to drain the ricotta in a fine mesh sieve overnight in the refrigerator. The texture of the ricotta needs to be drier in order to be firm enough to fill the shells.

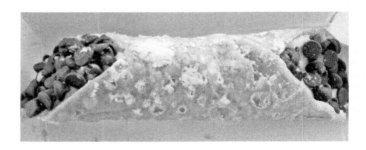

Homemade Ricotta Cheese

1 gallon whole milk

2 cups heavy cream

1 ½ tablespoons Kosher salt

½ cup white vinegar

Cheese cloth and strainer

Yields 4 cups or 2 pounds

Set a large fine mesh strainer over a deep bowl. Line the strainer with two layers of cheesecloth that overlap the sides of the strainer.

Pour the milk, heavy cream and salt into a stainless-steel pot. On medium heat, bring the milk up to 185 degrees. It will be steaming and gently simmering at the edges. Keep stirring occasionally so that the bottom does not scorch.

Once it reaches 185, stir in the vinegar, lower the heat to medium-low and cook for 2 more minutes. Turn off the heat and allow the mixture to stand for 10 minutes until it curdles. It will separate into thick parts floating on the top (the curds) and milky liquid parts (the whey). Use a large spoon to scoop the solids from the surface and place into the strainer lined with cheesecloth. Discard the liquid whey.

The longer you let the mixture drain, the thicker the ricotta (1 hour for moister cheese; 2 hours or overnight in the refrigerator for thicker cheese). Cover the ricotta with the overlapping cheesecloth. Discard the whey in the bottom of the bowl and refrigerate the entire bowl and strainer. Cover with plastic wrap.

After it has chilled for a few hours or overnight, transfer the ricotta to a bowl, unwrap the cheesecloth and discard. Use immediately or store in an airtight container in the refrigerator for 5 days.

Tiramisu

Filling:

8 ounces heavy whipping cream

⅓ cup powdered sugar

8 ounces mascarpone cheese, cold

1 cup pastry cream (see recipe)

Cookie Layer:

2 dozen Savoiardi cookies (hard lady fingers)

⅔ cup strongly brewed coffee

1 tablespoon instant coffee

⅓ cup "coffee liquor"

4 ounces dark chocolate bar, coarsely grated

In a mixer fitted with a whisk, whip the heavy cream and powdered sugar until stiff peaks are formed. Remove from bowl and refrigerate. In the same bowl on low speed, mix the pastry cream and the mascarpone until smooth. Fold in the whipped cream.

In an 8" or 9" square pan (preferably glass) arrange 6 cookies (sugar side up) in a single row on the bottom of the pan. Arrange 6 more cookies next to the first row. These cookies need to be cut in order to fit into the space. You will have two rows of cookies.

As soon as the coffee is brewed, mix in the instant coffee until dissolved and then add the coffee liquor. Pour into a shallow dish and **quickly** dip cookies in one at a time completely submerging, shaking and immediately removing. Place back into serving dish with sugar side up after dipping.

Spread 1/3 of the filling evenly over all of the dipped cookies. Sprinkle half of the grated chocolate over the entire surface.

For the second layer, repeat dipping more cookies. Try to line up the cookies in the same direction as the ones on the bottom layer. Spread the remaining filling on top of second layer of dipped cookies. Use an off-set spatula to evenly spread the filling.

Place remaining grated chocolate on a paper plate. Fold the paper plate in half. Starting in the center, sprinkle the grated chocolate in a few rows diagonally across the top.

Refrigerate a minimum of 4 hours or overnight before serving. Time is needed for the cookies to soften.

Pastry cream:

¾ cup whole milk

¼ cup sugar

1 tablespoon cornstarch

Pinch of salt

2 large egg yolks

1 teaspoon vanilla extract

1 tablespoon unsalted butter

Serves 9

Pour the milk into a heavy saucepan and heat the mixture over medium heat until it is hot and bubbles begin to form around the edge of the pan.

Place the sugar, cornstarch and salt in a bowl and whisk them together. Add the egg yolks and whisk the mixture until it is smooth and a pale yellow. Whisking constantly, slowly pour the hot milk into the yolk mixture. Return the mixture to the saucepan pouring through a sieve, to catch any lumps.

Return to a simmer over medium heat, whisking constantly, until a few bubbles burst on the surface and the mixture has thickened. Remove from heat and pour into another bowl. Add the vanilla and butter and stir together until butter has melted.

Place plastic wrap directly onto the cream and poke a few hole with the tip of a knife to let steam escape. Refrigerate.

This can be prepared 1-2 days in advance.

Italian Wedding Cake

Cake:

1 white cake mix

Whipped cream

2 cups heavy cream

½ cup powdered sugar

1 teaspoon vanilla extract

Filling:

2 pounds fresh strawberries, divided

8 ounces strawberry jam

Serves 12-15

For the cake
Preheat the oven to 350 degrees. Mix ingredients for the cake mix according to package directions.

Line a 9"x13"x2" glass pan with parchment paper. Paper should cover the bottom and go up the sides of the pan.

Pour the batter into the prepared cake pan. Bake until a toothpick inserted in the center comes out clean. Follow package directions for baking.

Let the cake rest in the pan until completely cool before inverting to a serving platter.

For the whipped cream
Pour the heavy cream into the mixer bowl fitted with a whisk. Add powdered sugar and vanilla. Beat at low speed until small bubbles form and increase the speed to medium and continue beating until the beaters leave a trail. Increase the speed to high and continue beating until the cream is smooth, thick, and forms stiff peaks. Refrigerate.

For the filling

Wash one pound of strawberries and dry them with paper towels. Reserve the other pound for the top of the cake. Cut off green stems and thinly slice strawberries into a bowl.

Place the cake on a serving platter. Remove the parchment paper. Slice the cake in half horizontally. Carefully slide a thin flexible plastic cutting board in between the 2 layers. With another thin flexible plastic cutting board placed on top, flip over the cake layer to expose the cut side.

Spread both cut sides with a thin layer of strawberry jam.

Spread a thin layer of whipped cream on top of the jam, on both cut layers.

Place a single layer of sliced strawberries on the bottom cake in the serving dish. Cover the entire cake with the sliced strawberries. Carefully line up with the flexible cutting board and flip the top cake (cut side) onto the bottom layer with strawberries.

Cover the top of the cake with the remaining whipped cream.

Pick out three of the best strawberries. Wash and reserve for the center of the cake. Wash, hull, dry and slice ½ pound of strawberries. To decorate the top of the cake, place sliced strawberries around the perimeter and reserved strawberries in the middle. Refrigerate before serving.

Chocolate Praline Cake

Cake:

1 dark chocolate cake mix

Praline Layer:

½ cup butter

⅓ cup half & half

½ cup brown sugar

½ teaspoon vanilla

¾ cup whole pecans, toasted and roughly chopped

Topping:

1 ½ cups heavy whipping cream, chilled

⅓ cup powdered sugar

1 teaspoon vanilla

grated chocolate

Serves 12-15

Cake

Mix ingredients for the cake mix according to package directions. Line a 9"x13"x2" pan with parchment paper. Paper should cover the bottom and go up the sides of the pan. You may also use two 9" round pans.

Caramel Layer

In a saucepan combine butter, half & half, brown sugar and vanilla. Stir on low heat just until butter melts and topping is a smooth sauce. Pour into the prepared pan. Make sure it coats the entire bottom of the pan. Sprinkle with the chopped pecans.

Carefully pour batter over pecan mixture in pan so that the caramel layer stays underneath the cake batter. Bake at 350 degrees for 29-33 minutes or until toothpick inserted comes out clean. **Cool only 5 minutes**. Take a knife and loosen sides. Place serving platter over top of cake pan. Turn the cake over and remove parchment paper. Scrape any nuts and/or caramel mixture off of the parchment paper and place on bare spots on the cake. Cool completely.

Topping

Pour the heavy cream into the mixer bowl fitted with a whisk. Add powdered sugar and vanilla. Beat at low speed until small bubbles form and increase the speed to medium; continue beating until the beaters leave a trail. Increase the speed to high and continue beating until the cream is smooth, thick, and forms stiff peaks.

To assemble one 9"x13"x2" cake, spread all of the whipped cream on top of the cake. Garnish with grated chocolate on top.

To assemble two 9" round cakes, place one cake layer praline side up on serving plate. Spread with half of the whipped cream. Top with other layer, praline side up. Spread top with remaining whipped cream. Garnish with grated chocolate on top.

Wine Cake

Cake

1 yellow cake mix

1 small package (3.625 ounce) instant vanilla pudding

1 teaspoon grated nutmeg

4 large eggs

¾ cup corn oil

¾ cup sherry wine

Topping:

light dusting of powdered sugar

Serves 12

Preheat oven to 350 degrees.

On medium speed, mix all of the cake ingredients in a mixer for 5 minutes. Pour into a 10" tube pan that has been greased and floured. Bake for 50 minutes or until a cake tester comes out clean.

Remove from oven and allow to cool slightly. Remove from pan and top with powdered sugar while it is still warm.

Pumpkin Roll

Cake:

3 large eggs

¾ cup sugar

⅔ cup pumpkin puree

1 teaspoon lemon juice

1 cup flour

1 teaspoon baking powder

½ teaspoon salt

2 teaspoons cinnamon

1 teaspoon ginger

½ teaspoon nutmeg

Filling:

½ cup heavy whipping cream

4 tablespoons butter, softened

1 cup powdered sugar

8 ounces cream cheese, room temperature

1 teaspoon vanilla

Serves 10-12

Cake

Beat eggs on high speed for 5 minutes. Add sugar gradually to eggs and continue to beat for 2 minutes. Stir the pumpkin and lemon juice into egg mixture. Stir together all the remaining ingredients and add to egg mixture. Stir on low just until incorporated.

Line a jelly roll pan (15"x10"x1" pan) with parchment paper so that it goes up all of the sides. Pour mixture into pan and level with an off-set spatula. Bake at 375 for 15 minutes or until cake springs back when lightly touched.

Remove from oven and allow to cool completely.

Filling

Whip the heavy cream until stiff peaks form. Remove the whipped cream to another bowl. Add the butter, powdered sugar and cream cheese to the work bowl. Mix on medium speed until batter is smooth. Add the whipped cream back to the filling and mix in the whipped cream.

Spread filling evenly on the entire cake with an off-set spatula. Use the parchment paper to help roll up the cake. Roll from the widest side and place on a serving platter with the seam side down.

Sprinkle with powdered sugar before serving.

Crustoli (Fried Dough)

2 ½ pounds Russet potatoes, with skins (6 medium sized)

¾ cup milk

1 package of yeast

1 tablespoon of sugar

5 cups flour, plus additional

1 teaspoon salt

3 tablespoons butter, softened

3 large eggs

32 ounces corn oil for frying

Glaze:

½ cup whole milk

4 tablespoons butter, melted

2 teaspoons vanilla

3 cups powdered sugar

Yields 48 doughnuts

Wash and boil potatoes with their skins for about 45-60 minutes or until fork can be inserted easily. Drain in a colander and allow to slightly cool. Peel skin and press through a potato ricer while still warm.

Heat milk to 110 degrees or lukewarm. Stir yeast and sugar into warm milk to dissolve. Let stand until foamy, about 5 minutes. Pour milk into a mixer and add potatoes, flour, salt, butter and eggs. Mix on low speed until a soft dough forms. More flour may be needed to form a soft dough that is not too sticky. Place in an oiled bowl and cover and let rise in a warm place for 2 hours or until doubled in volume.

Heat oil in a large 8 quart pan to 365 degrees. Punch down dough (it will be sticky) and with 2 tablespoons remove pieces of dough the size of a golf ball. Carefully drop the dough from the spoon into the hot oil (about 6) The crustoli will be all different shapes. Turn over dough and fry on the other side until golden. (Don't make them too big or they will not cook through.) Continue dropping more in after each batch is removed.

Prepare a jelly roll pan lined with paper towel and a wire rack on top. Remove golden crustoli and place on rack to drain.

Glaze:

Mix together milk, butter, vanilla and powdered sugar until the glaze is smooth. Add more powdered sugar if needed. Dip crustoli in the galze turning them until completely coated. Transfer with tongs to a rack set over waxed paper to dry. If desired, dredge in sugar instead of glazing.

Cream Puffs

Dough:

1 cup water

8 tablespoons butter

1 cup flour

4 large eggs

Pastry Cream Filling:

3 cups whole milk

Pinch of salt

1 vanilla bean, cut in half and seeds scraped out (optional)

¾ cup sugar (remove ¼ cup)

6 large egg yolks

6 tablespoons cornstarch

4 tablespoons butter

2 teaspoons vanilla

Yields 24 cream puffs

Preheat oven to 425 degrees.

Dough

Heat water and butter to a rolling boil. Keep the heat going and stir in flour vigorously until mixture forms a ball or leaves sides of pan. Remove from heat and cool for about 5 minutes. Transfer dough to a mixer and beat in eggs thoroughly, one at a time. Beat until smooth and dough forms a "V" when you lift the paddle out of the bowl. You may need an additional egg white.

Line 2 cookie sheets with parchment paper. Drop a full teaspoon of dough onto parchment paper about 1 ½" apart.

Place in the oven and bake for 15 minutes. Reduce oven temperature to 400 degrees and bake for an additional 25-30 minutes or until puffed, golden brown and dry. As soon as they come out of the oven, pierce a few times with a tooth pick. Allow to cool on a rack.

Filling

Pour the milk, salt, vanilla bean with the seeds and sugar into a saucepan and heat until simmering. Stir occasionally to dissolve the sugar.

Whisk egg yolks in a medium bowl until thoroughy combined. Add in the remaining ¼ cup of sugar and whisk until the sugar has begun to dissolve and the mixture is creamy. Whisk in the cornstarch until combined and the mixture turns pale yellow and thick.

When the milk mixture reaches a simmer, gradually whisk the milk into the yolk mixture to temper. Return the mixture to the saucepan pouring through a sieve, to catch the vanilla bean and any lumps. Return to a simmer over medium heat, whisking constantly, until a few bubbles burst on the surface and the mixture is thickened.

Pour into a medium bowl and whisk in butter and vanilla. Press plastic wrap directly onto the surface and poke a few hole with the tip of a knife to let steam escape. Refrigerate for at least 2 hours.

This can to be prepared up to 2 days in advance.

Assembly

Cut the top third off of the cream puff and save. Pull out any soft interior and fill with pastry cream. Place the lid back on top. Place on a serving tray. Repeat until the remaining cream puffs are filled. Sprinkle with powdered sugar. After filling, refrigerate up to 2 hours before serving.

Chocolate Mousse in Fillo Cups

Fillo Cups:

2 (1.9 ounce) packages mini fillo shells

Chocolate Mousse:

8 ounces semi-sweet chocolate

2 tablespoons slivered almonds, toasted

8 ounces heavy whipping cream

Topping:

8 ounces heavy whipping cream

¼ cup powdered sugar

1 ounces semi-sweet chocolate for curls

1 tablespoon slivered almonds, toasted

30 fresh raspberries

Yields 30 cups

Fillo Cups

Preheat oven to 350 degrees and bake shells for 5 minutes to crisp up. Allow to cool.

Chocolate Mousse

To toast slivered almonds, bake on a cookie sheet for 6-7 minutes at 350 degrees or until they are golden in color. Make sure it is completely cool before adding to the mousse.

Melt chocolate in a double boiler on stovetop or you can use the microwave for 50 seconds. Stir and cook for 15 seconds, until completely smooth. You may have to go for an additional 10 seconds. Add slivered almonds and stir. Allow to cool slightly.

Whip the heavy whipping cream in a mixer until stiff peaks are formed. Stir in ⅓ of the whipped cream into the chocolate rapidly. (This allows the chocolate to cool slowly so it won't seize and leave pieces of chocolate in the cream.) Fold the rest of the cream into the chocolate mixture until no white streaks remain. Spoon chocolate mixture into fillo cups.

Topping

Whip the cream and powdered sugar until stiff peaks form. Place in a pastry bag fitted with a large star tip and pipe stars on top and sprinkle almonds and top with a fresh raspberry.

Strawberry Mousse

1 pound of fresh strawberries

⅓ cup sugar

2 tablespoons lemon juice

8 ounces heavy whipping cream

1 package (6 ounces) fresh raspberries

1 package (6 ounces) fresh blueberries

3 additional strawberries for garnishing

1 package fresh mint

Serves 6

Wash, hull and cut the strawberries in half. Place in a food processor with sugar and lemon juice. Puree until smooth.

Whip the heavy cream in a mixer until thick. Pour the strawberry mixture into the whipped cream and mix on low until incorporated. Use a spatula to completely incorporate the whipped cream with the strawberry mixture.

For serving - use a small dessert cup (7-9 ounce) or small wine goblet.

Carefully spoon 3 ounces in the serving glass and place 2 raspberries and 6 blueberries. Carefully spoon another 3 ounces and top with 2 raspberries, 3 blueberries and a sprig of mint. On the side of the glass, press a strawberry cut in half with the stem attached. Refrigerate before serving.

Mini Cherry Cheesecake

Chocolate Sandwich Cookie Crust:

24 chocolate sandwich cookies, crushed (2 cups)

5 tablespoons butter, melted

Filling:

2 packages (8 ounces) cream cheese, softened

1 tablespoon vanilla extract

1 cup sugar

1 tablespoon cornstarch

16 ounces sour cream

3 large eggs

1 large egg yolk

Topping:

1 can (20 ounces) cherry pie filling

Yields 24 cheesecakes

Preheat the oven to 350 degrees. Line two standard 12-cup muffin pans with foil liners.

Chocolate Sandwich Cookie Crust

Mix crushed cookies and butter until crumbs are evenly coated with the butter. Spoon a full teaspoon into the bottom of each cupcake liner and press down to compact the crumbs.

Filling

In a mixer beat cream cheese, vanilla, sugar and cornstarch on medium speed until smooth. On low speed, add the sour cream and then the eggs one at a time just until the egg is mixed in. Do not overmix.

Spoon mixture to the top of each lined cheesecake. Bake for 15 minutes. The tops of the cheesecakes will slightly crack when they are done. Remove from oven and cool to room temperature. Chill overnight or for a few hours.

Topping

Spoon cherry pie filling (3 cherries) in the center of each cheesecake.

Mini Chocolate Cheesecake

Crust:

24 chocolate sandwich cookies with filling (2 cups)

5 tablespoons butter, melted

3 tablespoons toasted almonds, coarsely chopped

24 Foil cupcake liners

Filling:

2 packages (8 ounces) of cream cheese

1 tablespoon vanilla extract

1 cup sugar

1 tablespoon cornstarch

3 large eggs

1 large egg yolk

16 ounces sour cream

12 ounce bag of semi-sweet chocolate chips, melted

Ganache Topping:

½ cup heavy cream

¾ cup semi-sweet chocolate

6 ounce pkg. fresh raspberries

1 pkg. fresh mint

Yields 24 cheesecakes

Preheat the oven to 350 degrees. Line two standard 12-cup muffin pans with foil liners. Have all ingredients at room temperature.

Crust

Crush cookies to make crumbs. Place crumbs in a mixing bowl with the butter and almonds. Mix thoroughly. Set aside. Spoon a full teaspoon into the bottom of each cupcake liner and press down to compact the crumbs.

Filling

In a large bowl, beat cream cheese, vanilla, sugar and cornstarch with an electric mixer until smooth. Add eggs one at a time, mixing well after each addition. Stir in sour cream. Add melted chocolate and mix thoroughly.

Spoon mixture to the top of each lined cupcake. Bake for 15 minutes. The tops of the cheesecakes will slightly crack when they are done. Remove from oven and cool to room temperature. Chill overnight or for a few hours.

Topping

Heat cream in a small saucepan just until bubbles appear on the sides. Remove from heat and pour in chocolate chips. Swirl around until they are under the cream and let it sit for 2-3 minutes. Whisk together until it is smooth and glossy. Place in refrigerator for 10-15 minutes so that it thickens up.

Spread the ganache on the top of the cheesecakes and place on a platter.

Garnish with fresh raspberries (3 per cheesecake) and a mint leaf.

No Bake Cherry Cheesecake Pie

Granola-Nut Crust:

(One 9" pie pan)

1 cup granola cereal, toasted

¾ cup whole almonds, toasted

1 tablespoon brown sugar

3 tablespoons melted butter

Filling:

16 ounces (2 packages) of cream cheese, softened

⅔ cup sugar

1 teaspoon vanilla

1 cup heavy whipping cream, whipped

Topping:

1 can (20 ounce) cherry pie filling

Serves 8

Granola-Nut Crust

Preheat oven to 350 degrees. On a cookie sheet place granola and bake for 5-7 minutes. Remove granola to cool and place almonds on same cookie sheet and bake for 10-12 minutes or until toasted.

In a food processor pulse the granola, nuts and brown sugar until nuts are chopped into small crumbs. Combine ingredients with melted butter. 1 ⅓ to 1 ½ cups of crumbs are needed for one 9 inch pie crust. Press the crumbs evenly into the bottom and up the sides, forming an even crust. Chill until firm.

Filling & Assembly

Beat cream cheese, sugar and vanilla in a large bowl with electric mixer on medium speed until well blended. Gently fold in the whipped cream. Pour into the prepared crust.

Topping

Spoon cherry filling on top of the entire pie. Refrigerate before serving.

Sugar Cream Pie

Filling:

1 cup sugar

5 tablespoons flour

Pinch of salt

2 cups heavy whipping cream

1 cup half and half

2 large egg yolks

2 teaspoons vanilla extract

One 9″ unbaked pie crust

Serves 8

Prepare a jelly roll pan lined with foil or parchment paper.

Preheat oven to 350 degrees. Stir the sugar, flour and salt with a whisk. Add the heavy cream to the sugar/flour mixture until completely blended. Blend together the half and half and egg yolks and stir into the sugar/flour mixture. Just blend the mixture; do not beat it.

Place the unbaked pie crust into the prepared pan. Pour the filling into the unbaked pie crust.

Carefully transfer to the oven to bake for 75 minutes or until the top is golden and the filling still jiggles.

Allow to cool to room temperature and then refrigerate for two hours.

Fresh Strawberry Pie

Vanilla Sandwich Crust:

24 vanilla sandwich cookies, crushed (2 cups)

5 tablespoons butter, melted

Glaze:

1 pound strawberries, washed and hulled

¾ cup sugar

3 tablespoons cornstarch

Pinch of salt

1 tablespoon lemon juice

Filling:

2 pounds strawberries, washed, dried, hulled, and cut in half

Topping:

1 ½ cups heavy whipping cream, chilled

¼ cup powdered sugar

Yields 8 slices

Vanilla Sandwich Crust
Preheat oven to 375 degrees. Mix crushed cookies and butter in a 9" pie pan. Press into bottom and up sides of pan. Bake 7-9 minutes until set. Cool completely.

Glaze
In a food processor, puree 1 pound of strawberries until smooth and fully pureed, about 1 minute. Pour the puree into a small saucepan. Whisk the sugar, cornstarch and salt in a small bowl to combine, then whisk the mixture into the puree. Bring to a boil over medium heat, stirring constantly. When the mixture reaches a boil and is thickened to the consistency of pudding, remove from the heat. Stir in the lemon juice, and pour into another bowl to cool. Place in refrigerator until chilled. This can be made one day ahead.

Filling
Once strawberry glaze is cooled, combine with 2 pounds of strawberries cut in half. Pour into prebaked pie shell. Refrigerate until chilled.

Topping
Pour heavy whipping cream into the bowl and add powdered sugar. Beat at low speed until small bubbles form. Increase the speed to medium and continue beating until the beaters leave a trail. Increase the speed to high and continue beating until the cream is smooth, thick, and forms stiff peaks. Refrigerate until chilled.

Before serving, top each piece with whipped cream or spread the whipped cream over the entire pie.

Fresh Mixed Berry Pie

Granola-Nut Crust:

(One 9" pie pan)

1 cup granola, toasted

¾ cup whole almonds, toasted

1 tablespoon brown sugar

3 tablespoons melted butter

Glaze:

1 pound strawberries, hulled and cut in half

¾ cup sugar

3 tablespoons cornstarch

1 tablespoon lemon juice

Berry Filling:

1 pound strawberries, hulled and cut in half

1 pkg. (6 ounces) raspberries

1 pkg. (6 ounces) blackberries

1 pkg. (6 ounces) blueberries

Topping:

1 ½ cups heavy whipping cream, chilled

⅓ cup powdered sugar

2 teaspoons vanilla extract

Serves 8

Granola-Nut Crust

Preheat oven to 350 degrees. On a cookie sheet place granola and bake for 5-7 minutes. Remove granola to cool and place almonds on same cookie sheet and bake for 10-12 minutes or until toasted.
In a food processor pulse the nuts, granola and brown sugar until nuts are chopped into small crumbs. Pulse ingredients with melted butter. 1 ⅓ to 1 ½ cups of crumbs are needed for one 9" pie crust. Press the crumbs evenly into the bottom and up the sides, forming an even crust. Chill until firm.

Glaze

Place strawberries in a food processor and puree until smooth, about 1 minute. Pour the puree into a small saucepan. Whisk the sugar and cornstarch in a small bowl to combine, then whisk the mixture into the puree. Bring to a boil over medium heat, stirring constantly with a wooden spoon; when the mixture reaches a boil and is thickened to a consistency of pudding, remove from heat. Stir in the lemon juice, and refrigerate until chilled.

Berry Filling

Place the remaining berries in a large bowl. Combine glaze with berries gently tossing them together until the berries are coated. Pour into the cooled crust and distribute evenly into the pie pan. Loosely cover the pie with foil; refrigerate until chilled, about 2 hours. Serve with whipped cream.

Topping

Beat the heavy whipping cream and powdered sugar until the cream is smooth, thick and stiff peaks form. Serve on top of pie.

Banana Cream Pie

Crust:

6 ounces vanilla wafers, crushed
(2 cups)

5 tablespoons butter, melted

Pastry Cream Filling:

3 cups whole milk

Pinch of salt

¾ cup sugar (remove 3 tablespoons)

½ of a vanilla bean, split and
seeds scraped

6 large egg yolks

6 tablespoons cornstarch

4 tablespoons butter

2 teaspoons vanilla extract

Topping:

4-6 bananas, (firm but ripe)
peeled and cut into ½" thick
slices
1 ½ cups heavy whipping
cream, chilled
⅓ cup powdered sugar
1 teaspoon vanilla extract

Serves 8

Crust

Preheat oven to 375 degrees.

Mix crushed cookies and butter in a 9" pie pan. Press into bottom and up sides of pan. Bake 7-9 minutes until set. Cool completely.

Pastry Cream Filling

Pour the milk, salt, sugar, vanilla bean and seeds into a saucepan and heat until simmering. Stir occasionally to dissolve the sugar.

Whisk egg yolks in a medium bowl until thoroughly combined. Whisk in the remaining 3 tablespoons of sugar until the sugar has begun to dissolve and the mixture is creamy, about 15 seconds. Whisk in the cornstarch until combined and the mixture is pale yellow and thick.

Remove 1 cup of hot milk and whisk into the yolk mixture to temper. Pour the yolk mixture into the saucepan with the milk in it pouring through a sieve to catch any lumps. Return to a simmer over medium heat, whisking constantly, until a few bubbles burst on the surface and the mixture has thickened.

Pour into a medium bowl and whisk in butter and vanilla extract until butter has melted and pastry cream is silky.

Assembly

To assemble, spread 1 cup of the hot pastry cream over the bottom of the prepared crust smoothing with an off-set spatula. Arrange 2-3 cut bananas completely covering the cream, pressing down with your hands to pack them firmly. Cover bananas with 1 ½ cups of pastry cream. Repeat to build another layer with 2-3 cut bananas and cover with the remaining pastry cream.

Cover with plastic wrap and refrigerate until chilled, at least 1 hour. Place whipped cream topping on pie before serving.

Topping

Pour heavy whipping cream into the bowl, add powdered sugar and vanilla. Beat at low speed until small bubbles form. Increase the speed to medium and continue beating until the beaters leave a trail. Increase the speed to high and continue beating until the cream is smooth, thick, and forms stiff peaks.

Spread whipped cream on top of refrigerated banana cream pie.

Chocolate Almond Pie

Crust:

6 ounces graham crackers, crushed (2 cups)

5 tablespoons butter, melted

Filling:

8 ounce milk chocolate almond bar

¼ cup whole almonds, toasted

1 cup heavy whipping cream

Topping:

1 ½ cups heavy whipping cream, chilled

⅓ cup powdered sugar

1 teaspoon vanilla extract

Yields 8 slices

Pie Crust

Preheat oven to 375 degrees. Mix crushed graham crackers and butter in a 9" pie pan. Press into bottom and up sides of pan. Bake 7-9 minutes until set. Cool completely.

Filling

Melt chocolate bar in a double boiler on stovetop or you can use the microwave for 50 seconds. Stir and cook for 15 seconds. Stir until completely smooth. Fold in the whole almonds. You may have to go for an additional 10 seconds. Allow to cool slightly.

Whip the heavy whipping cream in a mixer until stiff peaks are formed. Quickly stir in ⅓ of the whipped cream into the chocolate. (This allows the chocolate to cool slowly so it won't seize and leave pieces of chocolate in the cream.)

Fold in the remaining whipped cream into the chocolate mixture until no white streaks are visible. Place into the prepared pan and cooled pie crust. Use an off-set spatula to smooth out the top.

Topping

Pour heavy whipping cream into the bowl and add powdered sugar. Beat at low speed until small bubbles form. Increase the speed to medium and continue beating until the beaters leave a trail. Increase the speed to high and continue beating until the cream is smooth, thick, and forms stiff peaks. Spread on top of pie. Garnish with grated chocolate and chopped toasted almonds.

Best Apple Pie

Dough:

2 ½ cups all-purpose flour

2 tablespoons sugar

1 teaspoon salt

2 sticks (16 tablespoons) butter, unsalted, cold and cubed

4 tablespoons sour cream

⅓ cup **ice** water

Filling:

6 large apples (3 kinds: Johna-gold, MacIntosh, Honeycrisp)

1 tablespoon lemon juice

1 teaspoon grated lemon zest

⅓ cup light brown sugar

⅓ cup sugar

3 tablespoons flour

1 teaspoon cinnamon

¼ teaspoon freshly grated nutmeg

¼ teaspoon salt

Topping:

1 egg white, beaten lightly

1 tablespoon coarse sugar, for sprinkling on top crust

Yields 8 slices

Dough

In a food processor using 6 one second pulses, combine the flour, sugar, salt and butter. Add the sour cream and ice water and use 5-6 one second pulses until the dough forms large clumps and no dry flour remains. (Add one tablespoons of ice water if dough is too dry and will not form a ball of dough.) Divide dough into 2 equal pieces. Flatten into 6" disks. Wrap in plastic and refrigerate for at least 1 hour or overnight.

Roll out one disk of dough larger than the 9" pie pan and gently push into the bottom and up the sides of the pan. Refrigerate until apple filling is assembled.

Move the oven rack to the lowest position. Line a jelly roll pan with foil. Preheat the oven to 425 degrees.

Filling

Peel, core and thinly slice the apples. Toss with the lemon juice and zest. Mix both sugars, flour, cinnamon, nutmeg and salt with the apples. Pour half of the apples into the bottom of the pie crust and press down so apples fit in. Pour in the remaining apples, mounding in the center. Press down again. Refrigerate.

Roll out the other disk. Place the second crust on top of the filling. Carefully roll and press the overlapping crust under the bottom crust, forming a thick edge. Crimp the edges of the crust down on the pan with a fork.

Topping

Brush the top crust with the egg white and sprinkle the coarse sugar. Vent the top with 4 slits about 2" long.

Bake for 30 minutes. Reduce oven temperature to 375 degrees. Bake for another 30 minutes. Remove and cool for a few hours.

Apple Cranberry Pie

1 unbaked 9" pie crust

Cranberry Filling:

2 cups fresh cranberries

½ cup sugar

¼ cup orange juice

¼ teaspoon ground cinnamon

¼ teaspoon salt

¼ cup water

Apple Filling:

5 large apples (Fuji, Johnagold, Pink Lady) 5 cups peeled and sliced

Zest of 1 orange

Juice of 1 orange

½ cup sugar

1 teaspoon cinnamon

3 tablespoons flour

Cranberry Filling

Bring the cranberries, sugar, orange juice, cinnamon and salt to a boil in a medium saucepan over medium-high heat. Cook, stirring occasionally and pressing the berries against the side of the pan, until the berries have completely broken down and the juice has thickened to a jamlike consistency (a wooden spoon scraped across the bottom should leave a clear trail that doesn't fill in), 10-12 minutes. Remove from the heat, stir in the water and cool to room temperature, about 30 minutes.

While the cranberries cool, adjust an oven rack to the lowest position, place a foil-lined rimmed baking sheet on the oven rack, and preheat the oven to 375 degrees.

Transfer the cooled cranberry mixture to the dough-lined pie pan and spread it into an even layer.

Apple Filling

Peel and slice apples. Add orange zest and juice. Toss to coat. Add sugar, cinnamon and flour. Mix all together.

Place the apple mixture on top of the cranberries. Push down and compress the apples.

Streusel Topping

½ cup packed brown sugar

½ cup all-purpose flour

½ teaspoon cinnamon

¼ teaspoon salt

4 tablespoons cold butter, cut into cubes

½ cup walnuts, roughly chopped

Serves 8

Streusel Topping

In a medium bowl, combine flour, sugar, cinnamon, and salt. Using a pastry blender or fork, cut in the butter until fine crumbs form. Toss in the walnuts.

Spread streusel topping over the top of the apples.

Place the pie on the preheated baking sheet and bake until the top is golden brown about 50-60 minutes.

Remove from oven and allow to cool for 2 hours.

Apple Sheet Pie

Pie Dough:

3 ¼ cups flour

1 teaspoon salt

½ cup plus 2 tablespoons vegetable shortening

14 tablespoons butter, cold and cut into ½" cubes

1 large egg yolk (save the egg white for brushing on top)

1 cup milk, cold

Filling:

3 pounds of assorted varieties of apples, peeled, cored and thinly sliced

⅓ cup sugar

⅓ cup brown sugar

1 teaspoon cinnamon

3 tablespoons flour

Glaze:

2 tablespoons soft butter

¾ cup powder sugar

3 tablespoons milk

½ teaspoon vanilla extract

Yields 24 squares

Pie Dough
Place flour, salt, shortening and butter into a food processor. Pulse for 6 (1 second) pulses to cut up the butter. Stop and add the egg yolk and milk and process for another 5 (1 second pulses) or until the dough just starts to come into a ball. If it is too dry, add 1 tablespoon of milk. Remove from food processor and divide into 2 pieces. Flatten the balls of dough into 7" disk and refrigerate for at least 1 hour. Roll out one of the disks to fit a jelly roll pan about 15x10x1" and refrigerate.

Filling
Mix all filling ingredients together to coat the apples. Place the apples evenly into the bottom of the prepared crust. Roll remaining dough for top crust.

Brush the egg white on top of crust before baking. Poke 6-7 slits on top for venting.

Preheat oven to 400 degrees and bake 45-50 minutes or until golden.

Glaze
Mix together until it is a smooth runny consistency. Add more milk if needed. Drizzle the glaze diagonally across the entire top as soon as it comes out of the oven.

Apple Crisp

Filling:

3 pounds of apples: golden delicious, pink lady, jonathan

⅓ cup sugar

⅓ cup brown sugar

1 teaspoon of cinnamon

3 tablespoons flour

Topping:

1 ½ cups flour

½ cup sugar

1 teaspoon baking powder

1 large egg (slightly beaten)

3 tablespoons melted butter
(slightly cooled) or corn oil

Serves 10

Filling
Peel, core and thinly slice apples into a large bowl. Place both sugars, cinnamon, and flour in the bowl with the apples. Mix together to coat the apples.

Pour apples into a 9"x13"x2" glass pan and flatten down the apples.

Topping
Stir dry ingredients together with a fork. Add beaten egg and melted butter and combine with a fork until ingredients are crumbly.

Sprinkle the topping mixture on top of the apples. Spread an even layer over all of the apples.

Bake at 375 for 50-60 minutes or until top is golden brown.

Cool completely and serve with vanilla ice cream.

Index

MEAT; BEEF, PORK, POULTRY & FISH

SOUP, SALAD & BREAD

Baby Greens with Fennel, Oranges, Dried Cherries & Slivered Almonds 28
Baby Greens with Mandarin Oranges, Dried Cranberries & Sliced Almonds 29
Banana Bread 33
Beef Barley Soup 20
Caprese Salad 31
Cheese Calzones 39
Cranberry Salad 32
Garlic Bread 36
Italian Wedding Soup 21
Minestrone (Vegetable Soup) 23
Minestrone with Potatoes, Cabbage & Rice 22
Mixed Bean Soup 26
Nonna's Chicken Soup 18
Pasta E Fagioli (Pasta & Beans) 24
Pasta Salad 27
Pizza 38
Potato Soup 25
Pumpkin Bread 34
Romaine Lettuce with Apples & Balsamic Vinaigrette 30
Soft Pretzels 37
Zucchini Bread 35

VEGETABLES

Broccoli 135
Cheesy Potatoes 142
Fresh Corn with Red Pepper 141
Fresh Green Beans 137
Green Beans with Pancetta 136
Green Peas with Shallots & Pancetta 140
Potatoes with Parmesan Cheese & Eggs 145
Roasted Potatoes 143
Roasted Root Vegetables with Gremolata 144
Sauteed Spinach 138
Swiss Chard, Potatoes & Beans 139
Twice Baked Potatoes 147
Vegetable Frittata 134
Yukon Gold Mashed Potatoes 146